William Wilkins

Songs of Study

William Wilkins
Songs of Study
ISBN/EAN: 9783337007058

Printed in Europe, USA, Canada, Australia, Japan

Cover: Foto ©Thomas Meinert / pixelio.de

More available books at **www.hansebooks.com**

BY
WILLIAM WILKINS
B.A. AND SCHOLAR, TRINITY COLLEGE, DUBLIN

> "Minds innocent and quiet take
> That for a hermitage"
> — LOVELACE

> "Yet, at the worst of the worst, books and a chamber remain"
> — CLOUGH

LONDON
C. KEGAN PAUL & CO., 1, PATERNOSTER SQUARE
1881

"But let your fair eyes and gentle wishes go with me to my trial."—As You Like It.

(The rights of translation and of reproduction are reserved.)

TO
MY BROTHER CHARLIE,
TO

ALL WHO LOVED HIM,

TO

THE UNIVERSITY HE LOVED.

Some of the poems in this volume have already appeared in serials, chiefly in *Kottabos*, a miscellany of Greek, Latin, and English verses, published every term in Dublin University. "Love Letter" and "In the Engine Shed" were included in a collection of poetry for recitation, edited in 1878 by Mr. John A. Jennings.

As once I set my songs before his face
    I set his name to-day before my songs ;
Because the sunshine of our study-place
    Came from his comradeship, which still prolongs
Its blessed sense beyond the graveyard murk,
And ever soothes me at my lonely work.

For I expect all day his entering,
    With steady eyes of hope, and merry smile
Fresh as the heather perfume, or the spring
    Of mountain streams, and potent to beguile
Dark thought, and prompt resolve to choose the best,
To follow and find and hold the worthiest :

Mercy, and justice, and the thrice-white fire
    Of scorn for slave and tyrant,—all the bright
Pure solaces of life, and high desire
    Above all things in heaven and earth for light ;
Such gods were his. Their temples yet remain,
Sacred for me, in every verdured lane

Between the mountain summits and the sea,
    Along our broad branch-waving country-side :
Wherever his free feet have gone with me
    In misty Irish sunshine far and wide,
Rejoicing in our youth with courage high,
And in the hills and cloudy-splendid sky.

In life and death I hold my brother dear,
    And bravely faithful to himself and me,
His deep love being all my atmosphere
    Till we lock hands in some new ecstasy;
Until new earth and heaven on me unfold
And our new comradeship transcend the old.

CONTENTS.

HEARTBEATS.

	PAGE
A LEAF OF SHAMROCK	3
T. C. D.	13
WHY	16
PALINGENESIS	18
DUBLIN COLLEGIANS	21
STUDY ON THE RIVER DODDER, NEAR DUBLIN	24
FRESHETS	28
GRATTAN BRIDGE, DUBLIN	30
FEUILLEMORTE	35
REVEILLON	36
REQUIESCAT	38
"HE GIVETH HIS BELOVED SLEEP"	40
A PLAYBILL	42
DEI GRATIA	43
PASTORAL	45
GOOD NIGHT	47

LANDSCAPES.

	PAGE
A March Whistle	51
Magazine Fort, Phœnix Park, Dublin	55
Night Air	56
August, 1878	57
Credo	58
Ludi	59
The Impassible	61
Actaeon	63
Ail Mavrisii	81

LOVERS.

To the Ideal	101
Easter Even	102
A Reminiscence	106
A Rejoinder (*Recast*)	107
Sketch	108
Godsend	110
A May Carol	112
Date Lilia	114
Recordemur	115
Gilliflower	119

CONTENTS.

	PAGE
PROXIMA—ULTIMA	121
A STORM SONG	122
A TRUE LOVER'S DITTY	123
MADONNA	124
LOVE LETTER	126
DEAD LEAVES	132
DISILLUSION	133
DOLLS	135
YEAR'S END	138
THE LAST TRYSTING	141
LEAVE-TAKING	143
A LATE PASSER	146
PIANO-EASEL	148
MAVOURNEEN	149
SONG	152
NOT AS YOU LIKE IT	153
A ROMANCE REOPENED	157
UNDER THE GILDING	161
HER WINDOW	163
LEUCONOË	167
A WINTER NIGHT	171
A FROSTFERN	174
GLADIATRIX	175
LADY BLANCHE'S AUSTRALIAN	177

VIGNETTES.

	PAGE
IN THE ENGINE SHED	185
MIRANDA	191
VESPERS	192
PICNIC	198
WHITE ROSES	200
PIA	202
THE DREAM OF PIA	206
EMIGRANT	210
TO THIS BOOK	212
ENVOI	216

ERRATUM.

Page 38, line 4 of quotation, *for* " ne " *read* " me."

VIGNETTES.

	PAGE
IN THE ENGINE SHED	185
MIRANDA	191
VESPERS	192
PICNIC	198
WHITE ROSES	200
PIA	202
THE DREAM OF PIA	

HEARTBEATS.

"Love is fellow-service."
CLOUGH.

"Arthur, the shapely, the tranquil, the strength-and-contentment diffusing."—CLOUGH.

"A new commandment I give unto you, That ye love one another."

A LEAF OF SHAMROCK.

WHILE my brother and I lived happily
In the worm-eaten storeys of Trinity,
I dreamed a dream as the morning dawned
On his innocent rest in the room beyond.

I dreamed of the room where late and early
We loved and studied, myself and Charlie,
The room that looked to the summer dawns
Over such greenness of boughs and lawns.

And under our wall that was built of books
The air was lit with a lady's looks,
Filling the place of our love and study
With melodied sense of maiden beauty.

A Muse-like being, she held herself
As tall as I by the mantel-shelf,
While Charlie sat in a place apart,
Holding us both in his inmost heart.

And over the depths of his brow and beard
The throat and breasts of a nymph appeared
Among carven primrose leaves,—a bust
Hewn by a dear hand now in dust.

Perchance there were more in our company,
But my dream was blessed to count these three.
—*Do* a youth and a maid suffice to each other?
—Ah! you know not the spirit of Charlie's brother.

And you know not the cheek of roseate pearl
Or the ivory soul of that Irish girl,
And the sanctuaries of snow-pure thought
In three student bosoms your soul knows not.

And you know not the dreams that were dreamed up
Where the gable is grey in middle air,   [there,
And you know not the wafts of unworldly ether
That Charlie and I have breathed together.—

—We talked in my dream, not a little moved,
Of Goldsmith, whose shy youth dwelt unloved
In our great rough College, and braved in vain
The time's harsh tempest of scorn and pain.

Then that maiden answered in earnest wise,
With her truthful soul in her eloquent eyes,
Of the worker's reward in his own pure will,
And the verdure of Erin made greener still

By his fame—in the minds of the few that count,
Who leaven the dull world's gross amount,
Who will lift up their faces in ages unscanned—
Saying, 'Erin, 'twas Goldsmith's, Foley's land!'—

"And though Goldsmith's ashes but few tears greet,
Lying trodden by London's uncaring feet;
Yet his image is fair in Foley's bronze,
And here for a glory to Erin's sons.

"And his perfect work has true Art's high strength
To pass like a light through the ages' length,
To shine in its place ever pure and bright,
The rival's despair, the disciple's delight.

"Therefore heed not cries of the chaffering mart,
But work thy work in the halls of Art;
With the heart's true love and the brain's true thought
Be the rock well hewn and the ore well wrought.

"Work truly thy work, whate'er it be,
For Erin and immortality,
And thy star, according to thy desert,
Shall shine in the cloudless heaven of Art."—

So she spoke in her Celtic eagerness,
With musical voice like a pure caress,
Enhancing the splendour of Goldsmith's doom,
Till I dared to dream it might light my tomb.

And Charlie smiled from his window-seat,
For our souls took joy when our eyes would meet,
And nothing seemed right till I talked it over
With my brother Charlie, my perfect lover.

Then was the course of my dreaming broken,
And Day bustled blithe in the world once more;
But that maiden's look and the words she had spoken
Long time in the heart of my heart I bore.

*   *   *   *   *

So the weeks went on, till my sleeping brain
Imaged in absence that room again,
With its busts and books, and its fresh air streaming
From Charlie's sleep to my place of dreaming:

The room where we met after every revel,
Where we laughed over chances of sport and travel;
The room we came back to from lonely lakes
In the brown wild hills, and from silver breaks

Of bright wild river and clear bleak shore,
And woodland glad of the wind's free roar;
The room that looked over such moonlit spaces,
The room never emptied of friendly faces;

The room that was bowered and based on love,
A temple to Tennyson, Browning, Clough;
The room that was rife with Shelley's verse,
And a chapel for Swinburne-reverencers;

The room by pure Imogen's faith made bright,
And Shakspere's dream of the midsummer night,
So sweet with the scents of Juliet's garden,
And merry with Rosalind's mirth in Arden;

The room where the jesters would come and go
In the smiles of our noble Bassanio;
The room so bright with the love in his eyes,
That I held my heart as his merchandise.—

And the Muse-like maiden was with us there,
The Shannon-breadth of her raven hair
By one eddy broken, and in its rift
Were shamrock and violet borne adrift;

Her skin, pure white as a seabird's feather;
Her lashes and brows, blue-black together
Like thunder-gloomed Irish mountains rainy;
Her eyes, clear dark as the pools of Slaney,

Dwelling softly with all a Muse's seeming
On mine, abashed at their tender beaming:
So beauteous beyond a mortal's possessing
And liquid with such appeal and blessing

That before her mouth of ripe-red spoke
Half out of my dreaming I awoke,
But her accents angelical, pure and small,
Flowed on like the plash of a waterfall.

"Through all the Future's field before me spread,
I see bright Song wind like a silver thread;
So through thy singing's passionate reach at Art
    I see thy heart,

"That loveth Beauty and is loved again,
That makes to bloom the wilderness of Pain,
That findeth bliss in misty breezes bland
    Of Ireland.

" As buds of April in the dewfall still
Ope pious petals on an Irish hill,
So let thy song in its meek chantry stand
    For Ireland."

Then laughing I—" Behold upon the wall,
Hogan's wild book,* a rebel battle-call,
The stormy-hearted singing, strangely grand,
    For Ireland.

" I drew first breath by the Ionian Sea,
That cools the winds of happy Arcady,
The sea whence beauty rose to make Hellene
    This worldly scene.

---

* " Legends of Thomond," by Michael Hogan. M. H. Gill, Sackville Street, Dublin.

"Beauty I worship only. Be my doom
That boys and girls may bless me in my tomb,
And say, ' He loved—until things cold and null
  Grew beautiful.'

" Not all my blood is Erin's. Wherefore strive
To keep old feuds of race and creed alive?
No Irish dower have I of immense
  Fierce eloquence.

" Vengeance and Sorrow beam from Erin's eyes,
I shrink before their black intensities ;
And pass in spirit to a higher land
  Than Ireland,

" Where for harsh drops of tears and gall, I taste
Nectar elysian, plenteous even to waste,
Brought by the godlike young immortal—Keats—
  From happy seats

" Where I would hope to kneel beside a door
Of that high court that sitteth evermore,
Where Milton, Marlow, Herrick, Shelley meet
  At Shakspere's feet ;

" Where I may hear pure Spenser's voice awhile,
And see old Chaucer smile his dear sly smile ;
Grave Wordsworth rapt upon the hills and streams,
  While Coleridge dreams."

" Yet Shakspere," said she, " is so great,—like God
With marvellous love and wisdom crowned and shod.
Think you his mighty merry heart knows naught
        Of Goldsmith's thought?

" Think you the godlike brother of all men born
Can hold sweet Mangan or bright Moore in scorn?
Think you his hand is slackened nor returns
        The grasp of Burns?

" Doubt not that even as aweless Byron stands
Flattered by favour at great Shakspere's hands,
So—lulled and loving—slumbers Irish ire
        In Shakspere's choir.

" Wherefore no doubt let enter in thine heart,
For Erin's art thou even as thou art,
And Shakspere loves the whole wide brotherhood
        Of human blood.—

" Hast thou not taken joy in Irish air,
And found our laughing Irish maids most fair;
Hast thou not seen their guileless eyes express
        Fair messages

" Of noble fellowship and upward aim?
And was his not an Irish face that came
Lighting the torpid darkness of thy youth
        Unto Life's truth?

"Hast thou not seen our sunsets gold and red
Fire city and haven and lone mountain head?
Hast thou not watched Ovocan glade and lawn
    Awake at dawn?

"Hast thou found greener glens than Glenmalure,
Or Glenismole's pure depths beneath Kippure?
Or thinkest thou some fairer way to pass
    Than Glenmacnass?

"Forgettest thou that gorge where with a cry
White Pollinass vaults out eternally
To those twin lakes deep-shadowed by the bluff
    Of grand Lugduff?

"Or that moon-haunted, hidden valley-end
Where Avonmore's young thronging streams descend
Their mighty magic stair of bliss and awe
    To Luggelaw?—

"From heavenly peak to diamond stream's fresh lip
Have brotherly love and artist fellowship
In storm and sun with thee gone hand in hand
    In Ireland.

"Wherefore to Irish smiles and scenes belongs
The sweetness given thee to fill thy songs,
So wear thou ever, in gladness and in grief,
    The shamrock leaf."—

I woke, and the mountain streams were loud,
And the mountain pines in the night-wind bowed,
And the farms were asleep in the muffling dark,
And as yet was no note from cock or lark.

And Charlie was sleeping, alive and well,
In the place where it was our delight to dwell;
With his blood's pure tune in untroubled bars,
And his windows wide to the lawns and stars.

*   *   *   *   *

Then the weeks, with excitement and action rife,
Went hurrying past in the dream of Life,
In street and study, despair and glee,
Playing their grim tragi-comedy;

Till upon thick darkness intolerable,
That folded all I had loved so well,
Came ghostlike the maid's pure look of mission
And suasive accents of soft monition—

To stir in my heart, that I thought was dead,
A sob of loving and lowlihead,
As my shipwreck of songs at her word I gave
To the sad green land of my hero's grave.

T. C. D.

Up here I sleep in the hawthorn scent :
    It swims through my windows from lawn to lawn,
While June's first nights with their deep content
    Possess my spirit from dusk to dawn.

I lying here, alone, a king,
    In the centre of pleasances green and sweet ;
Hearing the treetops murmuring,
    Hearing the far-away sounds of the street ;

With only to lean o'er the garden bed
    To see steadfast Jupiter shine in the south,
To see Arcturus hang overhead,
    And the stillness of spars o'er the river-mouth.

Eastward, westward—spread in the dark
    An acre of grass, an acre of daisies :
Northward, a square ; to the south, a park ;
    Mine is the midmost of pleasant places.

Hence I can see, as the midnight wears,
    The first blue tides of the morning steal
Between shores of cloud, among fleets of stars,
    Blanching the coigns of the Campanile

And all the divine repose that looms
    Through the College courts as the sweet hours go :
Palatial piles and their cloistered glooms,
    And dormer, and terrace, and portico.

While the sealike city is laid asleep,
    No motion or sound in its mountain heights
Of dark vast waves, or its furrows deep
    Sown with the lines of unnumbered lights,

Till the blue turns grey, and the grey turns gold,
    And the sea and land taste the new day's breath ;
And I hear the joys of the young morn told
    By the wakening birds in the boughs beneath :

And thus in the city I scarcely sigh
    For hollows that eglantines perfume,
And speedwells make like an under-sky
    Peering through clouds of chestnut bloom :

For I know my part in the treasure-trove
    Of the glad green meads where the June winds roam,

As I knew the looks of my fair first love,
    As I know the shapes of our hills at home.

And so I sleep in the hawthorn scent
    That dwells with me here like a haunting passion,
And so in the city I wait content
    While the time draws on to the long vacation.

1877.

WHY.

Three paces from our College door,
    The air flows round me unconfined;
    And, looking up, I bathe my mind
In the sweet heaven arching o'er.
    Blue, black, or grey as it may be.
    I love it always utterly
And feel my life to it belongs.

And that is why I make my songs.

I sing, for wheresoe'er I am
    If I but turn my thoughts apart,
    I fill the goblet of my heart
With tides of beauty clear and calm,
    Drawn from a source that lies far off
    Where human cares are lost in Love.
Unto that Love my life belongs.

And that is why I make my songs.

I sing, for wheresoe'er I walk
    By field, or stream, or windy grove,
    My thronging thoughts within me talk
Of others needing help and love;
    Of cheering sun, and soothing shade,
    Of courage—that is truest aid,
    I give them what to me belongs.

    And that is why I make my songs.

I sing, for all the noble dead
    Whose dust has budded into flowers,
    Would brighten these poor thoughts of ours
With trust and love and lowlihead.
    They lie in quiet clear and deep,
    And as they slumber we shall sleep,
    And our despairs—for them are wrongs.

    And that is why I make my songs.

PALINGENESIS.

WITH what sweet bread is my spirit fed?
   Of what wild wells hath it drunken to-day,
That I feel my blood like a Spring-swol'n flood,
   And my being a-tiptoe—merry with May?
Though I saw last night in my own closed room,
   As I thought upon what was dead and gone,
   The carols of songtide lost in moan,
And the glory of youth in gloom.

Ah! lamp and table, and rows of books,
   And all the untidy litter of study,
You hush not the sound of the rushing brooks,
   You blot not the tints of the sunset ruddy.
Never a problem puzzles the elves;
   The cuckoo's grammar is conned with ease;
And up on the lonely mountain-shelves
   Troubles are kissed away by the breeze.

PALINGENESIS.

I am escaped in the early Summer
    To plant free feet in the quickened green,
Among the deep hills a pale new-comer—
    One faded thing in a flowered ravine,
Where the swallow swoops and the brown bee settles,
    And cool streams murmur among young fern,
And dew lies cool upon primrose petals,
    And grief is a dark hour overworn.

High on the head of unnumbered winters,
    Bare to the blast and the burning noon—
Up where the topmost pinnacle splinters
    To fragments, bleached by the rain and sun—
Where the sky bends round like a vacant chamber,
    Curtained about with silken grey,
We came over shingle and scarp to clamber
    Up from the valley-land golden-gay.

Haze flowed below like a river of marble,
    Peaks peeped up, and between them gleamed
Shimmering stretches of broad sea-purple,
    Tarnished far as the sea-wind streamed.
Far away southward the shore went winding,
    Amber-sanded and edged with white,
And the inland distance flashed with a blinding
Lattice of lakes in the noontide light.

Many and many a golden rafter
    Sunset shot from the brown hill-wall;
Down we sprang with our merriest laughter,
    Mocking the far-away throstle's call,
Until at length, beneath whispering arches
    Of the cool young beechen wood,
We stood hushed, while the soft bough-surges
    Filled the soul with the solitude.

So all ills for a while are over,
    On to the end of the world I see
Rich, rich miles of the bright furze-cover—
    Balmy reaches of grass-clad lea.
So, new-filled with the life of Nature,
    I step, deep-breathed, through the sunset glow,
And my pulse keeps time to a marching measure
    Played by fifers of long ago.

Slieve-Gullion, Co. Armagh, 1874.

DUBLIN COLLEGIANS.

THEATRE ROYAL, 27*th November,* 1876.

How the blood in the young veins bounces expectantly—near and far :
For the playbill to-night announces the new Shaksperean Star,
Who is now for his trial nerving to the rising orchestral strain ;
For *Hamlet's* the piece, and Irving is to play us the Royal Dane.

What joy ere I press my mattress ! what chatter all round where I sit !
The noctivagant student head-dress being rife to-night in the Pit.
To " the Dress," if you come for flirtation— which is all very well in its way—
But the Pit is the student's station, when he really comes for the play.*

* See note, p. 25.

And the overture swells as it shouldn't, with our jesting
  and quip and quirk;
"Now mock me not, fellow-student, what make you
  from Wittenberg?"
"Oh! I make from electrostatics;" "And I from our
  training-boat;"
And another from Mathematics, and others from Jebb
  and Grote.

From divinity, hockey, dissections, foot-ball, philosophy—pshaw!
Peace to your glum recollections of Logic, and Latin,
  and Law.
And peace to the hospitals, measured by cramped
  limbs here gathered in—
Where Christians are killed, or are ushered crying—
  into a world of sin.

And Beauty, in bright exaltation o'er the joyous Babel,
  is met
By the wondering, mute adoration of the skilfully
  masked lorgnette;
And then eyes rove aloft to the ceiling and the galleries tier on tier—
A-dream in the violins' pealing, in the flutings, tender
  and clear.

We dream of the lips and the tresses, the jewels and
 fragrance and lace,
The colours of exquisite dresses, the faultless contour
 of a face,
A soul that our spirit goes seeking on pinions of perfume and sound—
We start wide awake without speaking as a hat rolls
 away on the ground.

The overture streams to conclusion, and hovers, and
 flutters, and clings;
The voices yet rise in confusion—when, lo! as a little
 bell rings,
The music dies, and the clappings die as a breaker
 dies on the shore;
And the curtain goes up on the midnight sky from the
 platform at Elsinore.

STUDY ON THE RIVER DODDER,*
NEAR DUBLIN.

The lovely sky is seen half-bare,
   The calm, bright river past us flows;
December holds the evening air
   As fairest fingers hold a rose,

So light, so sweet the touch of chill
   On clear green mead and winding tide;
The brown trees on the height are still,
   Nor mourn their plumy summer pride.

We feel the quiet Sunday time
   Sink to the heart. Though far away
Be bells that ring the vesper chime,
   The landscape, restful, bids to pray

* Between Rathgar Bridge and the gateway of Rathfarnham Castle.

As the heart prays without the lips'
    Weak words,—even as before our feet
The unruffled water, dreaming, slips
    From glassy sheet to glassy sheet.

We know this place. The poplar lone
    A tall, dark pillar—but it gleams
By moonlight,—the white arch of stone,
    The open green between the streams,

The gateway grey—amongst the trees
    That sweep between us and the south,
The cascade's murmur on the breeze,
    The low bridge at the brooklet's mouth,—

We know them all. They show to us
    The dearness of a dozen years ;
Twined memories multitudinous
    Of happy smiles, of bitter tears.

Rock-seated on the river's brink
    In sabbath twilight, strange is it
To watch the cool full stream, and think
    Of last night—of the excited Pit *

---

* Of the historic Theatre Royal, Hawkins Street — since destroyed by fire—but on the "College Night," 1876, filled by our fellow-students. The "Pit" came up to the orchestra in the old theatre, there being no fauteuils.

Filled with our lusty College crew,
   Red-ribboned, loud in Irving's praise,—
Young Hamlet full before our view,
   To haunt us till our latest days.

Breathless we watched him move and muse.
   The gilding and the gas were lost
Out of our minds. Who would peruse
   The imperfections of the Ghost,

Or shovings-on of Elsinore towers,
   While Irving held us by a spell?
A thousand hearts were tranced with ours,
   A thousand bosoms rose and fell

With Hamlet's sigh, with Hamlet's jest.
   The house was rapt. The galleries high
Leaned listening heads. The actor paced,
   Bearing the praise of every eye.

And after the great play was played,
   After the uproar of acclaim
That through the sleeping city brayed
   Its fanfare of the player's fame,

I grasped the fine-wrought, eloquent hand,
   I talked with Hamlet, friendliest-voiced;
Anon he took the table-end,
   The healths went round, and we rejoiced,

And the great heart's great gratitude
  For loving homage nobly won
And freely given, seemed more good
  To pledge, than aught beneath the sun.

Indeed, well-pleasing was the feast
  That filled the flying hours of night;
But now—this river's argent breast,
  The pale, sweet sky, the tender light,

Steal on the sense, and drink the soul;
  The clear west opens, calm and broad;
The deep peace deepens, and the whole
  Stirred spirit nestles up to God.

10*th December*, 1876.

FRESHETS.

The snows break up; and to the fields and hedges
    The spring her green flame sets;
And in the wintriest lane the tired eye catches
    Rare joy from violets:

Touches of God's divine relenting fingers
    Along the desolate ways,
Hope's coy tint glancing from these meekest bringers
    Of mournful strength and praise.

O my young hero in Life's earnest story,
    This spring you will not wake
To see with me the starry primrose-glory
    On bank and fallow break.

You will not hear the flooded streamlets breasting
    Their curves of turf and sand,
Nor see the daffodil—the wind's playmate—cresting
    The slopes of open land.—

—Will he not know this springtime how I miss him?
    How, as I sink to sleep,
The wild tears well with all my old "God bless him,"
    And how I wake to weep

Lest that mysterious country which he enters
  Should be as marred as this
With Doubt and Want, and plague and ghastly winters,
  And all that is not bliss?

Lest there, as here, an hour's ingenuous error
  Should, like a curse, remain
Fertile in daily shame and nightly terror
  And bootless rage and pain.

Lest, while despairingly I wait and waver
  With aching heart and brow,
He moaneth, smitten down in brave endeavour,
  "O for my brother now!"

And so I weep and weep, till I remember
  That if at all he be,
Then all brave hearts of true celestial temper
  Must love him utterly,

And God will be more near than in the frozen
  Foul town by the cold bay,
Where our hearts break, though violet-leaves be chosen
  To deck the rimy clay.—

O Death, best blessing sent us by Our Father,
  Balm for all aches and frets,
Would brother and brother slept in thy peace together
  Under the violets.

GRATTAN BRIDGE, DUBLIN.

From bright Glenaspinkin's wild dingle
    The mountain tides, flashing and free,
Sweep down to the city, to mingle
    At length with the tides of the sea:
Rushing under these well-trodden arches
    With throbs of a turbulent pulse,
While over the war of the surges
    Hang hundreds and hundreds of gulls.

Fine heads, and fine feet, and fine pinions,
    Poised high in the sunshiny air:
Pure creatures of purer dominions,
    Flown in to our foulness and care
With a sea-gust of Summer, that scatters
    The dust-laden smoke of the street,
And o'er the sick face of the waters
    Blows world-wide the ocean-breath sweet.

GRATTAN BRIDGE, DUBLIN.

O sea-mews, why come without warning
    To charm and unsteady my brain,
With the blue-and-gold burst of the morning,
    And flood of the hill-gathered rain?
O sea-mews, ye seem in your whiteness
    The unbodied souls of the blest
Passing by—a dear presence of brightness
    Come here to me out of its rest!

For here stood adoring together
    One night—in the summer gone by,
After tempest—myself and my brother,
    (The glad stars like tears in the sky
Of rapture and splendour and union—
    Of spirits by union sublime,)
Lost deep in transcendent communion
    Though we knew not it was the last time.

The west was a pale field of azure
    Slow-deepening (for sunset was done),
White-veiled with stray clouds—like the vesture
    Of bathers gone down with the sun,
Leaving scarfs from the limbs of proud maidens
    Strewn round, and by arch winds uncurled
On the shore of those seas of cool radiance
    That wash the bright ends of the world.

We strolled by the quayage and bridges
    In the tenderest time of the night ;
While throbbed in the clear river-reaches
    The freshet's and sea-tide's full height.
And this was the path my thoughts rolled in
    While deepened the evening divine :—
" I would not think the whole world too golden
    To give to this comrade of mine."

O God, am I robbed of his presence ?
    Do cold grasses thicken above
The sleep of that fair-growing essence
    Of all human power and love ?
Shall I reach him no more—save by loosing
    My hold upon all he held dear,
By quenching all action, and choosing
    The dreamless repose of the bier ?

O, better the grave-moss rain-sated,
    The weather-worn, mouldering stone,
Than to rot in the Life that he hated
    Inactive, unknowing, unknown !
O, better sharp Death's passing anguish,
    Than to wait without labour or aim,
Unloved and unloving, to languish
    And know but our bareness and shame.

GRATTAN BRIDGE, DUBLIN.

Far under the bridge-ledge of iron
    The ebbing sea-tide hurries down,
A-gleam—like a huge dying siren
    Whose white limbs and azure eyes drown
In tangles of giantess tresses
    Wild-eddying, twisted with snakes—
Writhing black in an agony that hisses
    And rears in the white water-breaks.

All the gliding death-spectacle glimmers,
    Far-stretching in lustre and gloom;
The drowned phantom beckons and shimmers,
    Deep-bosomed, broad-browed as the tomb.
O the cold of those anodyne kisses
    Plunged over my forehead and face;
And the opiate, killing caresses
    Of that down-dragging, mighty embrace!

The swift sun dispels her dead body;
    The sea mews float up with a cry.
Brave hold upon life is plain duty,
    Though deep be the pure bliss—to die;
And though yon vast shuddering spectre
    Of the city's corruption and crime,
Have given our beloved for nectar
    The poisonous fume of her slime.

In wild Glenaspinkin's green valley
    The din of the mountain cascades
Ever pours through the silences holy
    Where fern-plumes illumine the shades;
And oak-boughs and ash-boughs arch leafy
    O'er the chant's fragrant swellings and lulls,
Though hearts be so hopeless and heavy
    Down here, on the bridge with the gulls.

FEUILLEMORTE.

In the dreary College the days grow short,
While the dead leaf shivers along the court :
There is change—there is death—in the boughs and skies,
And the quick tears flash in my wearied eyes ;

Though I hold my grief as a thing reproved
That would sadden the daring of souls he loved.
Yet amid their speech comes the sense of death,
And I think of him, blessing him under my breath.

For " Ah ! " I have said to him, heart to heart,
" We have much to learn when our pathways part,
Launching forth from a love of such might and right.
Untainted by aught of the parasite."

And so, though his thoughts were so glad and brave.
I bear in the wounds of my soul his grave :
And so, though his brother and mine be by,
My heart—that would help—rots inwardly

With a sickening pang of ghastly stress,
While the day drags deathward its weariness ;
And my sight is with deluging thick tears drowned.
As the dead leaves shiver along the ground.

REVEILLON.

We thronged through the frost at midnight,—
    While the dean and the dons all slept,
And only the stars and moonlight
    Their watch o'er the stillness kept,—
For a great wild midnight revel
    Of a noisy College-boy horde,
Where the jest met the hundred-throated
    Vast laughter-storm round the board.

Good cheer and good wine and whiskey,
    And a fire that roared up the flue,
And faces of youthful triumph,
    And faces half-maniac too ;
Tragic, heroic, angel,
    As ever were seen on earth—
But now sadness was lost in feasting,
    And thought in the crash of mirth.

O the tunes on the mad piano,
    And the soloing tenor sweet !
O the pealing farcical chorus,
    Awaking the empty street !

O the toasts and the cheers and speeches,
  With ambushing jests of flame !
O the time when they all rose shouting
  With bumpers brimmed at my name !

O, God bless the dear, dear College,
  And my dear wild bright compeers,
Who guessed not my thought as I faced them
  With eyes on fire with tears :
For I thought of a voice that echoed
  Beside me oft in that hall,
And the silent grave-mould sinking
  On the dearest face of them all.

REQUIESCAT.

> " Encore une autre fois décembre
> Va retourner le sablier,
> Le présent entre dans ma chambre
> Et ne dit en vain d'oublier."
>   T. GAUTIER, *Le Chateau du Souvenir.*

In the College here of the Holy Undivided Trinity,
Fast by the city and river, and flanked by the hills and sea—
The gracious garden of study Queen Elizabeth made to be—

I dreamed at my open window, in the night's cool afternoon,
When the courts and park were crowded with the verdure of early June,
And soft upon lawn and tree-top lay the luscious light of the moon,

As it slept on the wrinkled headlands, the horns of our azure bay;
As it fed at the feet of mountains the ripening slopes of hay;
As it fell on the still canals, and their lashers' white shattering spray.

And sanctified were our chambers, as Juliet's high-bowered nest,
By the slow deep regular breathing of a sleeper's perfect rest—
Of all the students I loved, this student I loved the best.

The midnight freshness and fragrance blew in by window and door,
And fluttered the page poetic that the sleeper dreamed once more,
And the sibylline leaves of Science lying scriptured on desk and floor.

Not a far-off wheel-clang or foot-beat, the listening ear to fill;
Till the morning star flashed splendid through the yellow moonlight still,
And I lifted my dropped dear Gautier from the dewy window-sill.

*

The dream that I dreamed had ending, like the city silence deep.
To-day o'er the huckstering Babel, methinks, the angels weep,
And the door at my shoulder opes not on my darling's deeper sleep.

"HE GIVETH HIS BELOVED SLEEP."

The light in his window is darkened,
  The window set wide in air,
Where from carven clusters of primrose
  The nymph looks over the square,
In her curves of alabaster
  Eternally pure and fair.

The light in his window is darkened,—
  Though lovely her brow and breast,
Though the punctual dawn and sunset
  Have failed not from east or west,
His courage and patience are finished,
  And he is asleep and at rest.

Ah ! dear, be thy slumber unfevered,
  And thornless and glareless thy bed ;
Nor phantom of passion disquiet
  The calm that enmantles thine head,
But the slaking thick darkness forgetful
  About thee be heavily shed.

Nor moans of our wounded, nor weeping—
　　Howe'er we be weary at heart—
Make throb that true breast with our anguish,
　　Make mutter those lips at our smart:
In the march and the battle of living,
　　Not again, O beloved, have part.

If conquest were thine, and old bounteous
　　Frank-laughing defiance of ill,
The hearts that beat time to thy triumphs
　　Were yet as the pulse of thy will;
But the peace beyond all understanding,
　　Dear heart, is more bountiful still.

So the lights in thy windows are darkened—
　　Wide windows to east and to west—
And the quiet forget-me-not blossoms
　　With heart's-eases over thy breast,
And grief is assuaged by the whisper
　　That thou art asleep and at rest.

A PLAYBILL.

The Pit and the horseshoes o'er it
    Had smiles for their happy pave,
And over them surged at seasons
    Clear laughter's musical wave,
And it seemed, as I heard them laughing,
    As though I lay in my grave.

And so strange it seemed in my grave-rest,
    That the song at the foot-lights trilled,
That eyes had the same old brightness
    And the old laugh was unstilled,
That the old jest had the old relish
    And the empty places were filled.

Yet it soothed me to know in my grave-rest
    That the young were so bright and brave,
That the world could spare the broken
    Dead hearts that it could not save,
That there still was light and laughter
    Although I lay in my grave.

DEI GRATIA.

When hawthorn boughs begin to bud
   In eager green along the way,
And merry songsters toss a flood
   Of melody from spray to spray,
And in the budded branches play
    The little winds, not chill or loud,
    But, softly lifted, softly bowed,
Making the perches rock and sway;
     Then, gladsome as the lamb and lark,
      I break from grievous thoughts away,—
    Forget what's wrong, forget what's dark,
     And see the whole world good and gay.

When pearly skies break up in blue,
   Raining out milky, misty gold,
And all the sweet land through and through
   Is filled with pleasure manifold
   Of growth and light and music bold,

To close the wound and cure the smart,
And strengthen all the thankful heart
　In joyful praises dawnward rolled;
　　Then meekly as the milkmaids bring
　　　Their primrose posies pure and cold,
　　My soul grows happier—thinking Spring
　　　The smile of him beneath the mould.

PASTORAL.

We were four upon Easter evening
  Where these four fair valleys part,
The Goldmine vale, and the Aughrim,
  And Ovoca, and Glenart.

And we came to this very hostel,
  As now, amid evening hymns
Of the crooning woodland cushats,
  And the answering rush of streams.

We had come with the choiring waters
  Through the chapels of budding glades,
From their waking where Kevin worshipped—
  In white chorister-cascades.

And seaward, still chanting, chanting,
  As we paused by this wood-clad height,
The tides rolled, mixed with the moonrise,
  And kissed by the cherishing night.

We were four, by the benediction
    And bliss of the time imbued,
By the gleaming of branching waters,
    And the darkness of wood and wood.

We were two wrote missives to maidens
    At the time of the birth of stars;
We were two who pondered in silence
    Amid incense-rings of cigars;

We were four, for that sacred season,
    In a world that was calm and pure,
Made bright with hope and remembrance,
    And peace too sweet to endure.

We were four—who to-night are scattered
    With each one his thorn to grieve,
Although flowers and frondage and bird-song
    Abound for the Whitsun Eve;

We were four—who to-night are scattered
    On the currents of change and scathe,
And three are sad, for the fourth one
    Is in sight of the hostel—Death.

Though it seems but an hour since we rested
    Where these four fair valleys part—
The Goldmine vale, and the Aughrim,
    And Ovoca, and Glenart.

1880.

GOOD NIGHT.

When in my bed my limbs I lay,
    And feel the chillness of the sheets.
I think upon the graveyard clay
    Whose bridal clasp each creature meets :
    The coffin couch of shrouded sweets,
Where I shall sleep by night and day.

LANDSCAPES.

"O the wild green hollows full of heart's-ease.
  O the fragrant places where birds quire ;
  O the silence that is deeper than all language,
  And the cool that overpasses all desire!"

A MARCH WHISTLE.

The north wind blows across ridge and river,
   The pine-crest reels at his furious charge;
In the topmost woodland he roystereth ever,
   And high o'er the valley he flies at large.
     But ere he sweeps up the next bare hill,
     He whirls the wild rain, spattering chill
On cheeks that flush and on lips that quiver
   To hail the herald of lusty March.

The sea-channel spumes as the vast blast crashes,
   And up on the green cape springs the spray;
The billow leaps and the mad surf lashes
   Along the curve of the seething bay;
     And out at the lighthouse-point, the light
     Gleams like a star on the glooming night,
And ruddily over the wan surge flashes
   The levelled glare of its fiery ray.

But the storm will be well overblown to-morrow,
    And slowly will sink the swollen waves;
The new morn's verdure and breath will borrow
    A wild, fresh charm from this gust that raves:
        The sky and the heart from this day forth
        Will brighten, in spite of the blustering north;
For the joy of the young Spring soothes all sorrow,
    As daisies overgrow last year's graves.

The iron Winter is past and over,
    And mad March revels in glorious glee;
And the golden kingcup and purple clover
    Will soon embroider the deep-grassed lea:
        The primrose buds under holt and hedge,
        And forget-me-not amid sheltering sedge,
And the cool full freshet, a singing rover,
    Gushes along through the vales to sea.

The snows are gone, and the sharp sleet showers
    Will mildlier drive o'er the deepening green,
And the little speedwell and strawberry flowers
    In place of these daffodils will be seen.
        And the wild birds ever in glen and grove,
        Will carol to nested mates their love;
And ever will multiply with the hours,
    Pale primroses in the deep ravine.

A MARCH WHISTLE.

And the sky will be blue over hill and hollow
  And city and masted river-mouth,
And the mellow cuckoo and swift-winged swallow
  Will soon be here again from the south.
    And the lark will rise from the dewy lawn
    Chiding in music the lingering dawn;
And sooner and sooner the morn will follow,
  And every day will have joyful growth.

The dark tall wood, and bush and bramble,
  Light young whispering leaves will fledge;
And lambs will bleat, and with gleeful gambol
  Pass and repass by the coppice edge.
    And frosts will fail in the happy valleys,
    And blue-bells bloom and the dell's frail lilies;
And humming the gold-zoned bee will ramble,
  And bright mists float by the red hill's ledge.

And the moon will shine with her maiden splendour
  On mount and marsh and on mead and shore,
And the growth of the genial month shall render
  Much tribute rich to the Spring's fair store;
    For buds will open and flowers be born,
    And over the upland the late-sown corn
Shall thrive, though its paly shoots be tender,
  And vernal blooms shall be more and more.

And as the gladdening season advances
  Even the old will forbear to be sad ;
Sunshine bright in the stream-shallow dances—
  We will escape from the painful and bad.
    Love will range with his bow and quiver,
    And shoot sweet shafts (though at some, ah! never),
And there will be amorous sighs and glances
  Purely born between maid and lad.

So step out well over bent and heather,
  And set your face to the keen wind's bite,
With locks blown back in the bracing weather,
  And eye as the fledgling eaglet's bright
    For in cheek and limb the sharp-stung blood
    Flies like the mettlesome March wind rude—
Grey Winter is conquered altogether,
  And Spring exults in his infant might.

MAGAZINE FORT, PHŒNIX PARK, DUBLIN.

Inside its zigzag lines the little camp is asleep,
    Embalmed in the infinite breath of the greensward, the river, the stars.
    Round the staff the yellow leopards of England, weary of wars,
Curl and uncurl, to the murmurous voice of the greenwood deep.
On the lonely terrace their watch the shadowy sentinels keep:
    Each bayonet a spire of silver—high over the silvery jars
    Of the streamtide, swooning in starlight adown its foam-fretted bars
To the city, that lies in a shroud as of ashes under the steep.
    To the south are the hills everlasting; eastward, the sea-capes and isles;
    Inland the levels of emerald stretch for a hundred miles.

NIGHT AIR.

To the cape at our feet from the cape far away
On the changeful floor of the hill-girt bay
In a staircase of silver the moonbeams fall;
And outside the black sea lies like a wall.

Our life is varied—our life is bright
With noise and motion and tissued light,
All the restless days of our mortal breath;
But around are the hills and seas of death.

Alverno.

AUGUST, 1878.

(Adapted from the French of Emile Deschamps.)

WHEN the sun and wind have revelled here
    To sea-pink's rustle and sea-wave's chime,
When Killiney stands in the distance clear
    For another thousand years of time—
Some Irish or British Association,
    Picnicking, like us, in these shingles that rattle,
May talk of the past of our land and nation,
    Of Norman, and Dane, and King Brian's battle.
And across that age of the great world's growth
    This verse to some poet in love may say
That my love was staying a month at Howth,
    And that month for us went by like a day.
And this gorge will remember, and gaze to the south
    On the sunshiny hills and the breakers' play.

CREDO.

When roses hang by the meadow marges,
    And over the lawn the orchids bloom,
And June pours into the mountain gorges
    A deluge of golden gorse-blossom,—
I hold it better to range the coppice,
    And trace the stream through the ferny glen,
Than with dwindled breath in a dusty office
    To thumb the ledger and ply the pen.

When the branch is lost in the leaves that garb it,
    And heather flushes the mountain scar,
And scythes upgather the gorgeous carpet
    Flung over the landscape near and far,—
I trow it is sweeter to see the heaven,
    And rove in the sun with the birds and brooks,
Than with aching brows from dawn till even
    To pore and puzzle o'er crabbed books.

LUDI.

A CHORUSING circlet of childhood
    On flowers of carpeted wool,
A musical babel of laughter
    From blond baby heads beautiful
Round the bright little queen of the revel
    In her birthright of birth-night rule.

A tiny perfumed invitation
    Was sent us—for music and tea;
And the orphan who clung to my finger
    Laughed up in my face joyously
As he spelt out the motto, "Come early:"
    And here, welcomed early, were we.

And the sunset flowed over the children's
    Hunt-slipper and blind-man's buff;
And creatures, half-child and half-woman,
    Led far through the festal of love,
Half mad with delight of delighting,
    Till the heart, overblissed, said—"Enough!"

But dragoons, riding seaward that morning,
    Plashed deep through the mire of the plain :
Poor pawns on the chessboard of Europe ;
    A gloomy defile through the rain
For the helmets of brass and the mantles
    That shall rot in the fields of the slain.

And statesman sits puzzled by statesman
    And the grand royal battle-hounds gloat,
For the nations stand armed in the darkness
    And wonder if God taketh note
Of all the hands filled with leashed thunders,
    Of all the swords bent at each throat.

But the children played on until bedtime
    Their varying innocent play,
Without thought of God's toys—the statesmen,
    Without thought of peoples at bay ;
Going home in the hush of the twilight
    Through the branches and grasses of May.

THE IMPASSIBLE.

In Ovoca valley the wood and water
   Are dipt in a shimmering haze of light,
On the beach at Arklow the sand and water
   Flashes and sparkles in blue and white.
In Ovoca valley the woodbine-clusters
   Are hung in the wood like chandeliers,
In Arklow harbour the bright tide lustres
   The murmurous darkness under the piers.
In Ovoca valley the cart-boy listens—
   "Cuckoo, cuckoo"—through the brooding heat;
In the surge at Arklow the bather glistens
   A fairy—afloat at the green hill's feet.

The streams come down to Ovoca valley,
   Out of the distance, out of the hills;
From ledge to ledge falling musically,
   To a hundred lakes, in a million rills;
From stony teats of hugh Lugnaculliogh's,—
   And Mullacleevaun's enormous mass;
From Croghan and Douce and Carrowstick hollows,
   And purple summits o'er Glenmacnass;

From black Nahanagan, wilder Ouler,
　　And Luggelaw, walled with wood and rock;
From bright Lough Dan, spreading broader, fuller,
　　And the double darkness in Glendalough:
The streamlets repose and the streamlets rally,
　　And narrow and broaden down rapid and reach,
Till they mingle at last in Ovoca valley
　　With sound that abides like the scent of a peach.
But they flow in tune down Ovoca valley
　　Where miners tunnel the clear cliff's flank;
By coppice and meadow down musically,
　　And out in the offing to Arklow Bank.

In Ovoca valley a girl is singing
　　With glad thoughts fixed on her sailor frank,
While sand upon sand is the bright tide bringing
　　To bury that sailor on Arklow Bank.
The good ship sails and the glad girl singeth,
　　And sunshine is bright upon stream and sea,
The high hills gleam and the white wave springeth,
　　And stout is the sailor and filled with glee;
But when channel and valley in midnight slumber,
　　And rain rinses lawn and landing-place,
That ship shall be manned by a mermaid number
　　Whose kisses shall marble the mariner's face.
And the morn will be bright in Ovoca valley
　　Though the girl's heart break that her sailor sank,
And the wave will omit not a sparkling sally
　　In tossing his corse upon Arklow Bank.

ACTAEON.

"Sic illum fata ferebant."
Ovid, *Metamorphoses*, iii. 176.

It was on the mount Cithaeron, in the pale and misty morn,
That the hero, young Actaeon, sounded the hunter's horn.
Princeliest of pursuers of the flying roe was he,
Son of great Aristaeus and Theban Autonoë.
Oaklike in massy stature and carriage of kingly limb,
Lo the broad brave grace, and the fleet fine might of primal manhood in him;
Grandly browed as a sea-cliff with the curling waves at its base,
And its storm-haunted crest a tangle of deep ripe weeds and grass.
And many an Arcadian maiden thought not of a maiden's pride,
But looked on the youth with longing, and watched as he went, and sighed.

And Aegle had proffered a jewel that a queen might
 carefully keep,
For a favouring smile of the hunter, and a touch of
 his beardless lip;
But never on dame or damsel had his falcon glance
 made stay,
And he turned from the love-sick Aegle, and tossed
 her gifts away.

   For where was so soft a bower, or where so goodly
 a hall,
As the dell where the echoes listened to the noise of
 the waterfall?
And where was there cheek of woman as lovely to
 soul and sense
As the gracious hues of the woodlands in depths of
 the stately glens?
And where were there eyes or tresses as gloriously
 dark or bright
As the flood of the wild Alpheus as it poured from
 the lonely height?

   So the hero, young Actaeon, fled far from the
 girl-filled house,
To rove with the beamy spear-shaft through the
 budded forest boughs.
And sweeter than smiles of Aegle or sheen of her
 rippling hair
Were the heads of his great hounds fawning, or
 snuffing the morning air;

And to tread by the precipices that down from his
 feet shore clean;
And to mark where the dappled leopard was couched
 in the long ravine;
And to look on the eagle wheeling up peakward,
 and hear him scream;
And to plant strong steps in the meadows, and plash
 through the babbling stream,
And to hurl the spear in the thicket, and draw the
 bow in the glade,
And to rush on the foaming fury of the boar by the
 dogs embayed;
And ever in midland valley to smell the leaves and
 the grass,
Or the brine-scent blown o'er the headlands high up
 to the bare hill-pass,
Where lovelier far than Aegle or her eyes' bright
 witchery,
Was Morning, born of the marriage of silent Sky and
 Sea.

So the hunter, young Actaeon, to the mount
 Cithaeron came,
And blew his horn in the dank white morn to startle
 the sleeping game;
Nor thought, as the pealing echoes were clattered
 from crag to crag,
That Fate on his trace held him in chase, as a huge
 hound holds a stag.

By rock and by rift and runnel, by marsh and
  meadow and mound,
He went with his dogs beside him, and marvelled no
  game was found;
Till the length of the whole green gorge, and the grey
  cliffs gleaming on high,
Rang and re-echoed with horns and the musical
  hunting cry.
And the hounds broke out of the cover, all baying
  together in tune;
And the hart sprang panting before them along up
  the lawns dew-strewn.
And a bevy of buskined virgins, dove-breasted, broke
  from the bowers,
With spears half-poised for the hurling and tresses
  tangled with flowers:
Their lips, rose-ruddy, disparted to draw their delight-
  some breath
For the chase, and the cheer thereof ringing the
  rapture of dealing death—
The fine heads eagerly lifted, the pitiless fair eyes
  fixed;
The flower-fresh cheeks flushed flower-like,—rich lily,
  rich rose commixed;
The slender feet flying swiftly, the slight shapes rushing like reeds
When the Thracian breezes of Winter descend on the
  marshy meads;

So swept they along like music; and wildered Actaeon
    stood,
Till the last of the maiden rangers was lost in the
    leaning wood.

As a Bacchanal starts from slumber on snowy
    ridges remote,
To see o'er the peaks and gorges the silvery moon-
    beams float,
So the soul of the youth was smitten with wildest
    wonder through;
And a deadly tremor of madness through his quiver-
    ing members flew;
And a joy that was almost anguish took hold of his
    breast and brain,
And he nothing on earth regarded but to see the
    nymphs again;
Though the scorn of their arrowy glances should slay
    him a thousand ways,
He would die by their merciless sweetness with an
    open, adoring gaze.

And she, Diana, their leader, the queen of the
    greenwood glade,
The goddess of stainless maidens, herself a stainless
    maid;

Fair sister of sunbright Apollo, they twain being born
  at a birth,
Gold-haired children of Jove supreme, and lovers and
  lighteners of earth;
Phoebe, maiden majestical, sovereign lady most
  high;
Moon, more lovely, more chaste, than all the stars of
  the sky;
Cold as the dew on a flower and pure as the wings of
  a dove;
Divine—the rival of Venus, and more victorious than
  Love;
Ruler of mightiest waters, and couched in them night
  by night,
And soul of the sunless heaven, laving the world with
  light;
And edging the clouds and mountains with splendour,
  and tipping the trees,
And flying o'er lake and river with brighter feet than
  the breeze;
And at morn with kirtle and quiver a huntress by
  field and wood,
The swift overtaker, the certain smiter of hart and of
  pard pursued;
Hater of wantons, and shunner of sloth, and fleër of
  revels and feasts,
And scorner of man through the brutish in man, and
  lance-bearing slayer of beasts;

ACTAEON. 69

Enamoured of all the freshness that the lonely hills immure;
And Queen of Honour, and Patroness prayed to of women pure;
Modest maidenliness made perfect, immortal in virgin grace,
The young Actaeon would see her, and die beholding her face.

So the hunter wandered hapless, not caring to lift the spear,
But found not the racing maidens, nor heard in the woods their cheer;
And weary at last of seeking, he cast him adown to sleep,
Where joined a wood and a meadow in greenness heavy and deep
Of the watered Gargaphian valleys, that spread in the noonday heat
A welcome shelter for sun-scorched eyes, a rest for far-travelled feet.
So he dreamed; and lo, in a vision he saw a lovely place
With boughs overgloomed, and a river that fell down a rock's dark face
To a basin brimming with crystal, pebble-paved, mossy-quayed,
Filled with the dusky lustre and broken lights of the glade;

For though it was broad a spear-cast and mirrored a
  space of blue,
The tree-tops caught, and let fall, and caught the
  streams of sun pouring through;
And soothed was the scene with silence, and notes of
  birds far away,
And murmur of leaves, and the constant cadence of
  cascade spray.

And behold, there came through the thicket Diana,
  beautiful browed;
On her forehead a silver crescent that shone through a
  golden cloud.
And behind came her trooping sisters, unarming apace
  with glee,
And flinging buskin and girdle to rock and sheltering
  tree;
And fillets were loosed, and broadly were banner-like
  locks let fly;
And the dell was sown with snowflakes of swan-white
  shoulder and thigh.

Here a maiden, gliding downward, stopped breathless, as she set
Her small warm foot, an alighting bird, in the ferns
  forever wet.
And here, dishevelled, half covered in grasses, with
  timidest glance,

Sat one, as fearful to have unrinded so much hid
sweetness at once.
And here paced another, wondering, the sward feeling
strange to her palm,
And strange on her shrinking tenderness the forest's
breathing of balm.
And here another kneels musing, her slender beauty
all bare,
Fingering faintly the branches that mix with her long
brown hair.
A head like a glossy chestnut bends under the chestnut
frond,
While blushes like chestnut-blossom a face in the shade
beyond.
And thereby lingers a maiden, her stately shape dis-
arrayed,
Yet fain of the clothing dimness of scented, leaf-tinted
shade.
And here, disrobed, from the rushes twin laughing
sisters arise
Drawing the vagrant auburn from beaming bosom and
eyes.
And here on her innocent smoothness a maid watched
shimmer and spin
The sun-flecks rained from a breach far aloft where a
glory of gold broke in.
And here, where the slope was coated with close moss
daintily sleek,

A maid reclined on her elbow round, and touched it
  with hip and cheek.
And here, on the turf, one flushing at kiss of the delicate air,
Venus-like, rose from her billowing whirlpool of sea-
  dark hair.
And here, advancing together, dance maids like a wall
  of white,
Maid girded with arms of maidens, and dark locks
  flowing with bright;
Intercaressing delicious slim necks they move in tune,
  and their feet
Flutter o'er carpeting flowers, and, lily-like, mingle and
  meet.
Here, crouched on the brink, a damsel who peers, but
  suddenly swerves
To see in the tide beneath her the white of her soft
  full curves.
Here steps down a fair girl smiling, lightly borne as
  with wings,
Yet indeed like a panther stretching, and swift as a
  pard that springs,
She flies like a cloud of Summer, all nakedly bright
  from the wood,
And with round lovely arms high-tossing, Diana first
  cleaves the flood.
Through swirling luxurious water, clear-cold, made
  mad with her force,

ACTAEON.

With slight neck nervous, with long side shining, she
    holds her course.
And the rings of her plunge are broken, the spray of
    her splash borne back
By the milk-white flight of her maidens, who follow
    their mistress' track;
And the pool was gorged in an instant with beauty
    that sprang and swam,
And struck through the cisterned freshness with arm,
    and forehead, and ham.

  Here a face, pearl-dashed, rose-radiant, through the
    surge translucent hurls,
Towing by strong oar-pulses the silken raft of her curls,
Her hands making silvery fire of the water's voluptuous
    crests
That laugh at the touch of her shoulders and purr at
    the plunge of her breasts.
Here shoots a luminous body far down, skimming
    under the rocks,
And followed ever by turning trailing snakes of its
    golden locks.
And here sculls gently a maiden, her soft back bent
    for a keel,
With but lips and eyes over water, and sometimes a
    ruddering heel.
And here lies another, drifting, full-stretched in her
    snowy pride,

Enfolded from ear to ankle—a marble bar—in the tide.
And here, in the lustrous blackness that mirrors a wall of rock,
A swimmer eclipses her fulgent form that makes of the shade a mock.
And sinking in eddies that murmur for pleasure and swirl to her throat,
A damsel with spread arms paddles, and basks in the sunshine afloat.
And here, in a cove overshadowed, a soft shape beams from the gloom,
Censer-like shining, and—flower-like—set amid beds that perfume :
Lily of lilies, and tender mouth of the rose-bud's red and its mould,
And eyes of the violet's purple, and locks of the asphodel's gold.
And beside her the fluttering ripples, deliciously cool, caress
The polished waists of her sisters who wade to the landing-place.
And hard by, to a limpid shallow come three, in the depth to launch
A timid swimmer, their captive by ivory middle and haunch.
At wrist and at neck she catches. They bear her back from the bank ;

She struggles—their laughter echoes—those mischievous maidens dank.
Their arms interlace. Their whiteness is massed like a lily-brood.
They rear them, and fling them together with glee in the blissful flood;
And while yet the bubbles are bursting, each body and roguish face,
Rosed as with recent kisses, comes up from the river's embrace.

Now the hero, young Actaeon, heard the washing water lap
Round the knees and necks of maidens, and on dainty flank and pap,
And glad girlish voices mingling with the babble of the stream,
Yet was he but half delighted, knowing all was but a dream.
With the effort of a lifetime crammed into a moment's throes
He achieved his fate through torments, and—almost a god—arose
Flinging off the chains of slumber; nor had longer doubt or care,
Diana's pure suave contour, the young sunshine of her hair
Knowing:—even as a god knows the sweet pout of Hebe's mouth

When she brings the brimming vintage of no earthly
   vineyard's growth
For the gods to quaff together;—and his joy had
   naught of fear,
Breathing the Gargaphian breezes like a bridegroom's
   atmosphere;
But for lyres, and friendly voices, and warm scents of
   orchard bloom,
On Actaeon shone the everlasting glory of his doom.

   Earth's terrible high mane of the mountain naked-
      nesses,
The pastoral green plots in the piny glens' recesses,
The verdurous descent of the olive-girdled hills,
The generous air, the salving light, the voluble sweet
   rills,
The sunshine frank and flowing, the heaven overbowed
With unnumbered reefs and islands of tender-coloured
   cloud,
The cheerful fields, the bugling winds, the azure-
   gleaming bays,
The cordial of clear manhood, the joy of youthful
   days,
The temple-crested headlands that rise along the
   shore,—
Their lover, young Actaeon, left them all for evermore.
   For better than youthful manhood, and better than
      kingly sway,

ACTAEON.

And sweeter than happy wedlock, and dearer than shining Day,
Was to see the Queen Diana with his soul-filled maiden eyes,
And set for her sake his life at stake, and yield it a sacrifice,
That through all the unending ages the nations of men might know
How above ground a man was found to honour Diana so.

Thus to the thoughts of the hero disrobed was the virgin queen
As the moon disrobes to a glorified lake, dispelling the clouds between.
And the starlike mortal maidens inurn'd in the cool recess
Were too heavenly pure to blush himthought, or to know unbecomingness.
So the broad Actaeon thrust him through the thicket's emerald air,
And far through the ferns and frondage a tangled creek found there,
Where the oaks towered more majestic, the scents hung sweetlier sweet,
The grass throve thicker and thicker, as feeling Diana's feet.
Anemone, crocus, and pansy, in fragrant alleys untrod,

Bloomed ever lusher and lusher, as paving the path
of a god;
And hyacinth tufts in the covers made all the under-
growth blue
As the eyes of the streamlet peeping its Naiad-kept
lilies through.
And madness shone ever diviner in the hunter's ex-
pectant gaze,
And the air seemed rain-cooled about him, so fresh
were the forest ways
With youngest dew-diamonded herbage, and delicate-
burgeoning branches,
And deepening river-straits opening up to the waterfall's glances.

Suddenly brightened the water; the flowers of the
brim flushed rosier.
Suddenly looked Actaeon right into the sacred en-
closure.
Suddenly saw he a hundred tapering female shapes
lily pale,
Pureness of air and water and soul for their only veil.
And, fearless of male eyes gazing, Diana through
irised air
Showered the clinging crystal from free-tossing limbs
and hair.
The wave running over her insteps argent, Latona's
heaven-eyed daughter

ACTAEON.

Viewed her unrivalled whiteness beneath in the wavering water;
More regally high from the shoulder transparent than all her following vestals,
Statelily purest in virgin beauty, the noblest of the celestials;
Musing as muse the immortals upon their unutterable grace,
Her veined high brow bending forward, a brooding light in her face,
Watching the cooing waters that brightened and beamed as they passed her,
Glassing the nude refulgence of delectable alabaster.

So the hunter, young Actaeon, stood rapt for a little space
On the edge of the dell, and panted, his marvelling soul in his face;
While upon his temples noble did laurel and cypress meet;
Nor could he speak, nor retire, nor totter to fall at Phoebe's feet.
And lo, as the gods thus held him, there flashed a sudden storm
Of dazzling splendour and fearful, from Diana's dilated form,
Serene in high indignation, superb in haughtiest scorn,

Terrible in its beauty of deadliness heaven-born;
That the constellations of maidens shrank scared in
    the pools and nooks,
Nor dared encircle the awfulness of their incensed
    mistress' looks.
The small round neck lifting direly the exquisite
    menacing head,
The curving nostril, the steel-blue eyeball striking the
    gazer dead;
Rejecting his true, pure homage—though even her
    scorn was sweet;—
Smiting his life into darkness, and driving his dust
    from her feet.
Purity's anger, not pitying, even as python-slaying,
Bent the clear bow against innocence, fitting the arrow
    unstaying.
But Jove, the wielder of thunder, who smites for the
    righteous' sake,
Hid the young breath-despoiled hunter, and placed
    instead in the brake,
To appease the goddess, a roebuck, that bloodied the
    trampled ground,
Shot with Olympian arrows, and mangled by fangs of
    the hound.

AIL MAVRISH.

A MOUNTAIN IDYLL.

> "In youth when I did love, did love,
> O methought it was very sweet.
> * * * * *
> O a pit of clay for to be made
> For such a guest is meet."
> *Hamlet.*

> "What is Pyramus? a lover, or a tyrant?"
> "A lover, that kills himself most gallant for love."
> *A Midsummer Night's Dream.*

High up in Aughal, higher up than all
Smooth plots of culture in the straitening glens,
Up higher than the sunburnt cotter seeks
His coupled goats at eve, or herdsman comes
After strayed sheep, there is a barren tract
Peered down upon by Aughal's vast broad head:
A dreary, dreary hollow, in its midst
The lifeless oozing from a black wild lake
Plunged in a crevice of the mountain side;
The coarse grass flutters by the pale marsh moss,
The stunted heather starves between the stones,

And o'er it sails the eagle and the cloud.
Haply at dawn a fox may pause to lap,
Sated from prey, and howl and get him gone;
Leaving the place its utter loneliness
Of waste, and misty peaks, and pinewood strips,
And moory knolls that part and show the sea.

 Up to this desolation slowly came,
Amid the stillness of the August noon,
Ail Mavrish, wandering like an outcast soul.
His eyes had lost their light, his weary hands
Were void of rod and bow; and listlessly
He cast him on a cape of the lone tarn
And watched the gleaming water trickle down
The dark hill opposite, and heard the lake
Plash at its rocky isles and o'er the sand
Roll baby waves, and saw the water-weeds
Float, spreading loose and long. And so he mused
A space, and then up-gathering his limbs
He put his bonnet off, so that the breeze
Blew his high brow and ruffled the bronze locks
That ran in curls over his head like fern;
Then leaning back, he turned his earnest face
Up to the heaven, while his full-red mouth
Spake sadly on this wise:

      "O fair Lord Christ!
Who sittest with soft lengths of golden hair

Fallen round Thy face and on Thy shoulders curled
In Thine high bower of empyreal air—
O King majestic of the orbèd world,
Whose crown and countenance are lambent light !
Be merciful, my Master, to my woe.
Let me a little while lament, that so
I may not faint.   O Master, from Thine height
Unto me deign, and make my spirit strong
To speak to Thee of sorrow in the pause
Of mighty music of seraphic song ;
Nor let my foes destroy me with Thy laws.
Lord, as the leading angel bows his face,
And covers with his wings his pious brows,
Look from the glorious tumult of Thy house
Down to me lonely in this desert place.

" Ah ! holiest Lord, I am not in Thine eyes
Ail Mavrish, called of village maids most fair.
What boots to Thee a visage's device,
Or amber curls of much abounding hair ?
From the pure souls in Thy thrice-holy hall,
O Lord, look not on my unrighteousness,
I am no better than the common press,
Deserving at Thy hand no good at all
But rather stripes because we so transgress.
O, mark not, Lord, what evil I have done,
But pity me.   Thou knewest of my heart,
How it was turned (as ever to the sun

Turn the young flowers and the tender grass)
Wholly to Adiaber Lisnaglass,
From all things else aside and well apart:
Master, thou knowest how without demur
My soul went forth of me to follow her,
So fair she was—ah! Jesus Lord, so fair.
Thou knowest from Thy youth in Galilee
The mother-maid was not more fair than she,
Or those good saints that made Thy need their care.
So beautiful, my God, how beautiful
She was—and now a piece of rubbish dull.

"Thou knowest how her glamour on me came.
'Twas near the lowland harvest, and like flame
Pulsed the live air, and shone as silver doth.
Yet fell there one grey morning, as in sooth
It were October; saving that the trees
Were heavy with deep green, and blackbird's pipe
Rang mellow through them, and the tawny leas
Were everywhere unto the harvest ripe.
O Master, hearken; I was in the wood
Over the village. From the multitude
Of leafy lives my being drank much calm,
And I grew, Lord, as I but seldom am,
Devout and thankful. I was in Thine house,
Even in Thy presence. Ever through the boughs
Ran there a holy shudder to and fro;
And then uprose, with solemn swell and slow,

Over the brook's continual melody
The forest's hallelujah unto Thee.
—O merciful my Lord, Thou knowest that I
Am but Ail Mavrish, unto things devout
Given but little, and much grace without,
For Thou therein hast fashioned me awry;
But then with perfect heart I worshipped Thee,
And lo, Thine angel in the wood with me!

" Broke, steep and sheer, the pageant of the vale
Down through the foliage.   Afar off shone
The broken streak of the white waterfall,
A tremulous foaming staircase.   Thereupon
I heard soft laughter and a chirping voice
Behind the drooping branches of a beech.
So, looking forth after the pleasant noise
That tranced mine ears with what celestial speech,
I saw a tiny foot and outspread gown.
—There sat she in a sloping mead new-mown
Between her sisters, binding fresh-culled flowers
Wherewith her fragrant lap was overstrewn.
And as she wrought, she spake; and charmed the
    place.
—O God most high, the favour of her face
Thou knowest, being wise.   Thou madest it,
So wherefore should I, with my crazy wit
Praising amiss Thy sweet work, only mar.
There is no summer noon or evening star

Whose faultless beauty could compare with hers:
The fairest thing in all Thy universe
She was,—the very fairest, and now, Lord,
She moulders, covered by the churchyard sward.

"O God, O God, sustain me but an hour,
Then let me die when I have told Thee all:
The sun declines along the mountain wall,
Gilding this pool that I shall make my grave.
I have not left the strength to go afar
And seek Thy face through the red gate of war,
Or where the ship dies in the breaking wave.
The streams of Aughal shall my pale form lave,
Wrapt in cool mosses; and the mountain wind
Shall moan above me, crisping this lone pool.
So shall I cease, and naught be left behind
To tell the gossips how I played the fool
For a girl's love—I, darling of the glens—
Lost quite. My heirdom shall another have
And my possessions all be other men's!
But Thou, O Lord, be merciful, and save
My soul more pain. Thou know'st my heart must break,
I am so wholly wounded for her sake.
O bear me up, good Lord, that I may say
What I have never said until this day:
My love of Adiaber Lisnaglass.
So shall my soul be eased a little, and pass;

And Thou, good Lord, have pity of Thy grace
Upon mine anguish and mine evil case !

"O hearken, Lord. Thou sawest how I stood
There wondering on the margin of the wood,
While she with her fair sisters laughed and spoke,
Fingering the flowers. Presently there broke
A twig I leaned on, and her lustrous eyes
Leaped on me, and she flushed ; but I, flame-red,
Dizzy with pleasure and with shamed surprise,
Tottered forth to the maidens and there said
Lamest excuses—truth and lies, God wot
That eaves-dropping or spying I was not—
Unhingèd prate, in sooth I know not what.
For little Florise held by Einan's waist
And so severely eyed my floundering haste
With such serene blue orbs, that, faith ! I stopped,
A tingling fool. Then gentle Adiaber
(With female grace that was at highest in her)
In pity of my pain said, ' O fair youth,
For thine approach our thanks are due in sooth :
Rousing our truant thoughts thus civilly
Out of this pleasant nest where we have dropped.
We might have stayed here ever as you see,
Plaiting sweet garlands, feasting on the view
Of this thrice lovely valley, but for you.
Now, sent by Heaven, to our aid you come
To break our chains and point the pathway home.'

"What gracious words! I saw her lips and locks,
And smile so wondrous that I almost reeled
And fell before it in that happy field:
(O heart, be still; I sit on lichened rocks
Up here in Aughal, praying ere I die).
I offered rest and entertainment meet
For gentle strangers (never three so sweet
Came to our vale) in any cot hard by;
For heir, I said, of these long glens was I.
'Nay,' said sweet Adiaber, 'good youth, nay;
Thanks for thy courtesy! but we must not stay.
Direct us, prithee!' But so sweet she made
Even refusal, that I still essayed—
Till Einan joined against me, saying 'Nay'
With her grave dignity, so I gave way.

"I brought them through the woods and coppices,
Tipsied with Adiaber's graciousness.
Einan put off her stately elder mien,
And condescended like a gentle queen
To her beloved sister's playful mood;
And in a shady sylvan solitude,
Where dusky boughs the winding pathway spanned,
Florise crept up to me and took my hand.
But O! sweet Adiaber, brightly tressed
With richest auburn curls—— Thou knowest best,
O Lord, *her* beauty, and the matchless form
That now is eaten of the writhing worm.

"O God, sustain a while my bursting heart !
Thou knowest, when at last we came to part,
How courteously spake Einan, and how shyly
Looked up young Florise,—like a woodland lily
Nodding alone in early summer-time
In the green shadow of a spreading lime.
But Adiaber simply said, ' Farewell,'
And thanked me smilingly; so dared I tell
My thought, and asked a posy of her flowers.
Thereat she blushed, and gave me from her stores
This woodland posy, edged about with fern.
Lo now, poor faded leaf and shrivelled stem,
Yet presently I shall die kissing them.

"O Master, pity me beside this tarn !
—I watched the three departing hand in hand ;
Einan with rounded limb and swelling bust
And pale proud face that might the world command.
—Shapen and poised so queenly is her head
With its well-ordered load of raven hair,
That, were my sorrow known, it would be said
Einan's clear beauty is beyond compare.
O God, Thou knowest what is now but dust !
How marvellously graceful was *her* step !
The strait sloped shoulders, and the neck and bust ;
Lips, eyes, and hair, Thou fashionedst them forth—
Yea, all the treasures of her slender shape.—
There is no match for them in all the earth.

"O Master, Thou art good, but men are vile;
What evil thing should bar me from her smile
Whereof my hourly dream was, night and day?
I hoped to take the ancient feuds away,
And make all smooth with amity and goodwill,
In time, when I should rule the rugged glens
That run through Aughal's fastnesses immense
Wherever any land is habitable;
But then, because the feud ran rancorous
Between the house of Lisnaglass and us,
I held my peace and wrought my way alone.

"Thou knowest, Lord, what love this simple folk
Of dwellers in the glen all bear to me.
There is not any of them has made moan
Of country hardships, roof or fences broke
By flood or weather, unto whom I spoke
Not lovingly, or turned from wantonly.
They say that I am beauteous as of old
The heathen gods, of so divine a mould
Hast Thou made me for grace and strength and
 speed,
And so I am beloved; but indeed
It is not so, but for I gently speak
And love to kiss a curly child's red cheek,
Nor do men wrong, nor use my place amiss:
It is for this they love me—but for this,
Good Lord, and for no other thing it is.

And so, I said, my deeds and praise should soothe
All the old sores; and yet in mine own youth
I should see peace in all the country-side,
And woo sweet Adiaber to my bride,
And live in love with her and rule the glen.

"Alas! how evil are the hearts of men!
We came together, Lord, on the same day
To the same church, to kneel to Thee, and pray
'Our Father,' and to drink Thy sacred cup:
And yet our hearts were guileful, boiling up
With legendary hatred and deep wrath
Towards one another—save my heart and hers;
Thou knowest mine and gentle Adiaber's!

"The harvest went and came, and aftermath;
And shearing time and harvest came again.
And ever as the moon would wax or wane,
Or leaves came forth upon the sprays, or fell—
Her beauty grew almost intolerable
In splendour; and my love such joyaunce had
And growth, methought sometimes I was gone mad,
So glad my heart was, O fair Lord, so glad.

"Not as the hypocrites do I make sad
My visage, or quote saws in doleful chant.
Lenten behaviour is not much my wont,
Thou knowest, Lord, for I am wild and rude

In Thy pure sight, and have no whit of good.
So often, when the priest is mumbling prayer,
My eyes and thoughts go roaming otherwhere
Than they should do; but ever as I look
Einan's clear face is bent upon her book,
As rigidly as it were carven stone.
But Adiaber's, God wot, like mine own
Heeds not the handled matter overmuch.
—Was not her loveliness a righteous thing,
And virtue in her cheek's pure blossoming?
Yea, her sweet beauty better than much alms,
And sleepy rounds of prayers, and midnight psalms
Made by ill-favoured saints and hermits gaunt,
In places that grim spirits would love to haunt?
Ah! Lord, consider well how hard it were
To fix that angel head with glossiest hair
And eyes where played like sunshine in a stream
Quick thoughts as bright and vivid as a dream—
To fix them poring on a blotted page
Until the dazzled sight should blur and smutch:
Albeit Einan in her hermitage
Of staid calm thought could pray even as a nun.

"O good Lord, hearken till my tale be done;
When have I vexed Thee with my prayers before?
Thou knowest when my heart was often sore
For her dear sake, I did not weary Thee
With fretful plaints of shameless beggary,

But sought to work—and not to cross—Thy will.
Not even in the glen's high chancel still,
The holiest place for prayer that Thou hast given,
Shut round by sky and rocky mountain walls
And choirs on choirs of pines and waterfalls
Between the long blue lake and the blue heaven,—
Not even there my pain I basely eased,
Saying, 'God surely dwelleth here well pleased,
And hath too much of joy to frown or spurn
If I should beg what He would have me earn.'
And all that time Thou knewest all my thought,
And often saw mine eyes grow dim and hot
Because Thy hand refrained and gave me not.

"And, Lord, Thou knowest with her I justly dealt,
Nor let her dream the fever that I felt,
Lest she should pity and suffer all too soon.
I would not crave or steal her virgin boon,
But bravely bore my pain and held aloof.
Remember, Master, how I played my part
Lest any one should vex us with reproof:
Although my very life in her was set,
I only sought her with mine eyes and heart.
Yet was her smile, whene'er by chance we met,
And the enlivening of her beauteous eyes
Encountering mine own, a richer prize
Than in the spoil of palaces may be won.

"Thou knowest all things, Lord, both greatest and
    least,
And wherefore not that secret secretest
That troubleth a young maid's tender breast,
Bidding the joyous madcap Sport begone !
I saw the damsel's rich cheek falling pale,
And evermore her eyelashes' silk veil
Shaded the large orbs of her glorious eyes.
What shook that softest bosom with deep sighs,
And stayed her bounding step and innocent glance ;
And stole the smile of her sweet countenance
That gracious was to all, but unto me
A keener, clearer sweet than aught but love could be?

"Spring grew to May, and May went on to June,
With deepening glow of summer sunshine boon.
The plague was in the cities, and at eve
The muffled bells rang weirdly through the glens,
Calling to pray against the pestilence ;
And the great kirk's arched aisles could scarce receive
The throngs of worshippers from dale and down,
And frightened fliers from the stricken town.
Here prayed we purely for the smitten land :
Though no rank breath of sickness could withstand
The roaring winds of Aughal's rocky gorges ;
Yet, natheless, we knelt us in the churches
And prayed against the plague.
                      O that last night !

O God, be it remembered in Thy sight
When we rise up before Thee in Thy Day,
I from this lake, she from the churchyard clay;
And that red sun which Aughal thrusts before
Shall faint and die and shall be found no more;
Then to our suppliant souls Thy mercy show
And stand the blessèd cross 'twixt us and woe.

" The church was black throughout with kneeling
　　folk.
Scarce room where one might drop a sparrow broke
The dense, dark throng. The lights were burning
　　low
Round the vast image of the Crucified,
Yet flared sometimes and wavered to and fro
As the breeze freshened off the mountain side.
And then uprose with solemn swell and slow,
Like the hoarse moaning of the midnight sea,
The penitential wailing litany
Echoing far away along the glen:
A lamentation breaking out again
And yet again, that made the breath grow scant
For awe, there in the summer twilight pure.
And as the priests intoned the holy chant
To Thee whose mercy ever shall endure,
Grandly broke in like thunder now and then
The pause when all the people said 'Amen.'

"And she was there—
                    Thou sawest, O Lord God,
The fair flesh Thou hast bruised with Thy rod,
Cast down before Thee in its costly dress,
Mourning its small share of unrighteousness :
The white neck bowed until the last sleek tress
Fell off it, and the small hands tightly clasped;
And where the perfect face was pressed with tears,
Thou heardest, Lord, how brokenly was gasped
With sobs, *her* plaint—O good Lord !—Adiaber's.

"Thou knowest, indeed, what business took me
    then
Away from Aughal, and from her away,
And from the quiet of our long still glen
To be beyond the hills for many a day.—
Ah ! not so many, Lord; for then 'twas June,
And lo, there is the golden August moon
That shall not blanch before I be at rest
Within this polished brooch of Aughal's breast.—
And while my heart breaks in this mountain cove
All envy me a little amid their love
For wealth, and late great riches of goodwill
Won with such joy in handling of affairs
Discreetly—after my poor share of skill;
While the plague failed before the people's prayers,
And evermore came news from home that said
No sickness lurked in view of Aughal's head.

"But lo, I am come back, and there is one
Dead of the plague. Yea, Master, one alone—
A bloated corse under the churchyard sod:
Her wholesome sleek white body spotted o'er
With deathful green and livid—O Lord God!
Her fragrant lips only a loathsome sore:
Swelled up and foul that was so pure and sweet,
That all men speaking of her in the street
Are horror-struck, and say Thy ban was hers.—
O gentle Christ! Thy meek child Adiaber's!

"I am so stricken, Lord, that scarce could I
Drag my weak body up thus far to die,
Telling Thee of my love and of my woe.
I cannot bear the beautiful green glen
With wild streams welling from the rocky spurs
That start up here and there amongst the furze
Above the cotter's farms.
     What profits me
Lewd waste of women's lips unkissworthy,
When she—the pearl of womanhood—is low:
The maiden moon that lightened all my skies?
Thou, Lord, art gracious and not blind like men;
Judge us with mercy when we shall arise.
This chill night wind bites through me like a sword.
Pity my soul and Adiaber's, O Lord!"

LOVERS.

"Ah! years may come, and years may bring
The truth that is not bliss,
But will they bring another thing
That can compare with this?"
CLOUGH.

"O dear Ophelia, I am ill at these numbers, but that I love thee best, O most best, believe it."—*Hamlet*.

In endless procession from Eden,
Hand in hand, pair on pair,
Sweethearts : maiden and youth.
Falsehood, misfortune, tears,
Disenchantment, broken hearts.

TO THE IDEAL.

AH, may she find amid my verse,
    Above poor personal joy and pain,
Something to win a smile of hers
    And entrance at her heart to gain,
Some aspiration pure enough
To dwell an instant in her love;
Then I sum Life's iron and dross and gall,
And I count that instant worth it all.

EASTER EVEN.

Good night. Across the College quadrangles,
   O'er park, and lawn, and quiet cloisters fair,
Where meek-eyed, soft-stepped Meditation dwells,
   Deepens the cool grave twilight everywhere.
   High carven emblem, through the dusky air
Seen dimly, fades into the glowing gloom ;
   The rows of windows round about the square,
Merge into shadow until morning's bloom,
And all is hushed, and still, and lonely as the tomb.

Good night, good night. As thy beloved eyes,
   The young great stars look on me at this hour :
From deepening blue of holy western skies,
   One after one born into fullest power
   Of glorious purity. Like a summer shower
Come thoughts upon me, many, swift, and keen,
   Like mingled rain and sunshine, sweet and sour ;
Sweet—being of thyself, my fair child queen,
Yet sad almost as that sad saw—" It might have been."

Good night, good night; my thoughts take wing to thee
    Out of our town and mountain-circled bay,
Across rough leagues of hoarse and hoary sea
    And misty hills and landscapes, far away
    To thy dear vales that primroses inlay;
Night-mantled now, but beautiful as when
    I watched the moonbeam of the early May
Creep through them nightly, and the woody glen
Was wild with nightingales that closed to pipe again.

Stand close, my soul, within the garden gate,
    Where bows the clambering rose-tree at the door:
It may be she will sing, while thou dost wait,
    Some strain of holy sweetness—lingering o'er
    Notes that thou lovedst well in days of yore,
An evening hymn, perchance, to thee well known—
    O soul, how well! how precious evermore!—
Perchance thou wilt but catch a word—a tone;
Yet O, how rich a prize to thee by chance winds blown.

My lost first friend, what memories on me throng!
    The old quaint room comes round me by degrees,
And thou art sitting at thine evensong,
    Thy fingers wandering 'mongst harmonious keys,
    Thy clustering ringlets in sleek broideries
Upon thy gracious head: once more I hear
    Thy warbling of smooth-dittied symphonies,
While unseen choirs of angels, hovering near,
Join faint celestial echoes to thy vespers clear.

Ah, me! how often as the daylight failed
　　From Ulster mountain terraces, barren-brown,
And slowly westward the grey even trailed
　　O'er tree and mast and spire and farm and town,
Have I—across my books—o'er dale and down
Gazed at thee—heard thy sweet soft notes arise—
　　Mused on thy dark thick tresses richly strown
Over young neck and shoulder—met thine eyes
Filled with such liquid light of mute but glad surprise.

Or, dearest, as the summer sunset waned
　　On Leinster hills from Howth to far Kippure,—
Torn Dodder, by the bright sky dyed and veined,
　　Foaming down rocky channels evermore
　　To the blue bay of tawny-sanded shore,—
While in its vale the distant city lay
　　In haze and murmur, and the soft winds bore
Chimings of bells and scents of clover-hay,
Oft have I seen thee, sweet, and kissed thee far away.

Wafted along the dewy, cowslipped lanes,
　　Where hang the may's white, scented arches wide,
And waving honeysuckle's gilded trains,—
　　From pastures cool, where flocks lie unespied,
　　The night-air of thy quiet country-side
Blew freshly on my face, and I could see
　　The hamlet, and the looming church beside,
And the dear ivied cottage, that for me
Held treasure passing far all wealth of Araby.

The rustic English home, with tiles deep-mossed
    And garden round about hedged from the road,
And hospitable door by low beam crossed!
    Oft have I seen in dreams that fair abode,
    Oft seen how the wood fire at even glowed
On the brick hearth, and threw its ruddy glare
    O'er snowy wall and red floor all abroad,
And lit kind faces gathered smiling there,
And thine enchanted eyes and massy pure dark hair.

Good night, good night. Sleep soft, my tender dove,
    Curtained from fear of storm or any jar;
In everlasting guard of seraph love,
    And watched by maiden eyes of moon and star:
    Blessings upon thy rest I breathe afar,
Longing to send thee balmy slumber sweet,
    And haply some fair dream—that still we are
Frank playmates, amid happy chirp and bleat,
Pacing thy meads of joy with blithe unfettered feet.

A REMINISCENCE.

KISSING wan olive into red rose—
    Black earrings, black eyes, and white white teeth
Flashing about like pearls and sloes,
    As you laughed and struggled my lips beneath.—
Little slim body so clear and fine,
And little weak hands held fast by mine—
Little bright face as keen as wine,
    Do you remember? *I* shall till death.

Kissing wan olive into red rose—
    Like April flushing at once to June—
Kisses commencing on kisses' close,
    And laughter on laughter abounding boon.
You played me a trick at the garden ferry,
But paid me a forfeit sweet and merry
One sunny morning last January—
    Have you forgotten, my dear, so soon?

A REJOINDER (Recast).

You have made the wan olive redder than ever,
    With rhymes that remember a lawless kiss,
By the moss-grown garden and sparkling river,
    One morning a twelvemonth divides from this;
Clear little compliment, neat and fine,
And little blithe verses, made to be mine,
Little bright lines that blush like wine—
    How have you fashioned them, dear old quiz?

You have made the wan olive redder than ever
    It flushed to the pressure of kisses in fun.
The second atones for the first endeavour.
    Though blushes be deep in the morning sun.
I played you a trick by the garden ferry,
And have paid you forfeitures sweet and merry,
In frosty sunshines of January.—
    I shall not forget them,—and now—Have done.

SKETCH.

The rose-branch bowed at the window;
 The sun came streaming through
On the stars and squares of the pavement,
 Orange, and crimson, and blue;
Flashing white on the helmèd Pallas
 Of massy marble and rare,
And firing with golden the chestnut
 Of Agatha's waving hair.

The breeze of the summer morning
 Swept in from the lawn and lake,
To kiss her on lips and forehead,
 And bright eyes newly awake;
And to fondle her shapely shoulder,
 And girdle her slender waist,
And to hover round earring and ringlet,
 And the flowers she wore on her breast.

Her schoolfellow's far-sent missive
    Held captive her thoughts awhile;
She sped through the close crossed writing
    With a wondering slow half-smile,
As she stood by the broad hall-table,
    Nor dreamed of her girlish grace;
Her whole heart lost in her letter,
    As mine was lost on her face.

GODSEND.

She rose from her couch at dead of night,
In her sleeping garment loose and white;
    The hasp of the window she undid,
    The sash on its hinges inward slid,
    And the chill wind entered her bower unbid.

Her hair, as dark as the wetted earth,
Fell streaming down to her snowy girth;
    Forth she leaned, and her slippered foot
    On the dewy slab of the sill she put;
    And she clasped her hands and rested mute.

Up to the stars a space she gazed,
Her pure bright soul with her eyes upraised.
    Out of my body my soul arose
    To the worshipping beauty the fates disclose
    To my worshipping eyes,—and the sky's repose.

Behind her the chamber, closed and black ;
The river beneath, and the winding track
    In the laurelled cliff where I held my breath :
    About me the branches were still as death,
    And the glen as a stone that mouldereth.

I stood in a trance on the garden moss
Till she closed the sash with the sign of the cross.
    I signed the cross in the starlight bright.
    For methought I had seen the holiest sight,
    Since the Bethlehem angels carolled at night.

A MAY CAROL.

I SHALL see her to-day,
   No wonder the skies are blue,—
No wonder the world in its best array
   Flaunts as fashioned anew:
No wonder the world is at play, at play,
   In green and purple and gold,
For I shall see her to-day, to-day,
   Who is all my joy to behold.

I shall see her to-day,
   I woke with the joyful words,
And the blue sky laughed upon where I lay,
   With the twitter of leaves and birds,
And the soft winds brought me the scents of May,
   And the sun sent goldenest light
To say, I shall see her to-day, to-day,
   Who had filled my dreams all night!

A MAY CAROL.

The village will hold its festival,
    And the joy-bells joyously chime,
My darling is coming, my all, my all,
    The joy of the joyful time;
And the children will dance and the flags will fly,
    And all hearts with the music stir,
But the birds and the winds and the flowers and I
    Will have all our joys in her.

The earliest roses peep,
    For they know she will surely come,
And the lilac thicket, so sweet and deep,
    Puffs down to her fume on fume;
And the bluebells and lilies will all look up
    As she comes by the greenwood way,
Where primrose and violet linger in hope
    To see her,—to see her to-day.

I shall see her to-day,
    I dream of her night by night,
No wonder my blood makes holiday,
    And goes half mad with delight,—
No wonder the sunshine fills the air,
    And the whole wide world is gay,
For my love, my love, O! so fair, so fair,
    I shall see her to-day!

DATE LILIA.

How purely lovely !—Ah, give me lilies,
 Loveliest bells that the May shower wets.
Roses are lovely, but lovelier still is
 The lily half-hid among violets.
Forehead and ear and cheek are of lilies;
 Branch-dark her hair that the oval sets
Of her face—my world where not anything ill is;
 Her eyes are a pair of violets.

Lilies! violets! violets! lilies!
 Blue interlilied pure violets,
Dawn-bedewed in the dearest valleys
 Whose hollows the tarnishing sun forgets;—
My love is a lily of legioned lilies,
 Breathing the freshness of violets.

RECORDEMUR.

O CHAIR, that held her gracious shape
   For one short hour of happy rest,
   Remember how thou hast been blest,
Nor from thy hard heart let escape

How sisters came this afternoon
   When all the city swam with heat—
   Their maiden eyes and slender feet
In the great desert wearied soon.

Yea, She came to my reading-room,
   This bower of my dear-dreamed sleep
   With open windows buried deep
In ivy and laburnum-bloom;

This garden-gazing bed-chamber,
   The fortress of my childish joys,
   Now strewn with books, instead of toys,
And verses made from thoughts of her;

And maps that show the mountain path
   And stream where I am used to rove
   Moulding sweet ditties of my love
In praise of beauties that she hath.

But now—my solitude, that swarmed
   With hopes and sweet remembrances,
   By all her living loveliness
And presence angel-pure was charmed:

For through my matted ivy-boughs
   The summer fever cannot strike,
   Although the streets be oven-like,
And stifling our deserted house—

Whence all my kin some hours ago
   Took flight unto the breezy sea;
   But, till my love be there, for me
No joy is there, I said; and lo!

There comes a rustle on the stair,—
   A girlish step—a timid knock;
   But e'er my fingers touched the lock
My heart cried out that she was there,

And opening quickly, dizzy-glad,
   I met her splendid stately smile,
   Begging to rest a little while
And taste well-water in the shade.

And so I stood and ministered—
  Here in the window where she sat—
  And talked with her of this and that,
While the light wind her ringlet stirred.

And so amid my tumbled books
  And graceless shelves her beauty dwelt,
  And shining through my life I felt
The sacred luxury of her looks.

And here she laid her hat and gloves,
  And there she leaned her parasol ;—
  'Tis meet that I remember all,
For now this chamber is my love's—

Who sat in gentle stateliness,
  Framed in the window's green and brown,
  And watched her sister up and down
Forage at will, and at my glass

New clasp the band on her shining hair.
  Then I suddenly thought my dream to tell ;
  But my heart beat like an alarum bell,
And as I looked I did not dare—

She was so wholly beautiful,
  In girlish glory queenly sweet,
  With sister frankness so complete—
Here chatting with me in the cool :

Her soft bright ringlets loose and long,
  Her eyes reviving like twin flowers
  That taste the gelid April showers,
Her laughter like a linnet's song.

Behold, a wonder without end—
  The worshipper before the shrine
  And she who was for him divine
Prattling together, friend with friend!

Yea, surely. In my chamber calm
  Her graciousness made me rejoice;
  I drank the music of her voice;
I talked with her;—I touched her palm.

And she is gone. The evening wears,
  The west o'erflows with golden light.
  But I shall love her noon and night;
And thou, be chiefest of my chairs.

GILLIFLOWER.

Never a pool by the wayside,
  Never a cloud in the sky ;
Whirling down to the seaside
  Through the dust of July.

Foamy the four bay horses,
  Jolting the stale old coach.
Parched were the low grey gorses ;
  The meads were sunned overmuch.

A ridge that the heat shone hard on
  We crossed, and came in view
Of the shaded house, and the garden
  That treasures its sweets for you.

And eyes half-blinded and weary
  Were turned to the watered green,
To the murmuring oak-boughs cheery,
  The lawns with flowers between.

And I said, "I will watch her window
    Set wide to the summer air,
And my panting spirit will lean to
    The jasmine that clambers there."

You sat in the noonday coolness
    With midsummer fragrance fed:—
Your muslined bosom's fair fulness,
    The ribbon that bound your head;

Your smooth deep locks, gathered neatly,
    A fern in their dark silk nook;
Your ruby lips parted sweetly,
    Your calm blue eyes on your book.

You looked from your green-chased bower,
    Drawing back that I scarce could see;
But a hand like a woodbine flower
    Was waved—with a kiss for me.

That was all; for, lo, my pleasure
    Was gulfed in the high, thick trees:
But the ocean before spread azure,
    And I tasted the rich sea-breeze.

PROXIMA—ULTIMA.

Only to look on her lips
   Is to sink through all depths of despair.
Her name, as in prattle it slips—
   A glimpse of her up-gathered hair—
Sends all the blood to my heart
With the chill of a death-giving start;
   And a fiend's keen talons of ice,
Plunging deep in their malice divine,
   Take hold of my soul like a vice,
As I mutter, "She cannot be mine."

A STORM SONG.

Toss, tight boat, by the foam-covered bar ;
   Dip deep down in the jaws of the brine.
Fly, dark rack, across moon and star,
   Fly, and fly past.—My love is mine.
Storm-stricken cedars, reel on the height ;
   Hurled back, shudder, and pitch to the wind.
Swept by the beam of the moon's pale light,
   Lash, and loom grandly.—My love is kind.

Burst, O sea, on the sands of the shore ;
   Scream aloud. Fling up your wild arms white.
Grovel, and shriek to the strong wind's roar ;
   Peal up your cry through the pitiless night.
Blow, vast gale, over field and bay ;
   Over holt and hill whirl the rain and brine.
Ruin and wreck till returns the day ;
   Break, and be broken.—My love is mine.

A TRUE LOVER'S DITTY.

O PLEASANT bevy of bright gay girls
Who with silver laughter and sheeny curls,
And arch sweet glances, and gracious words,
Have soothed my journeying hitherto—
O fair sweet friends, I have done with you;
The nightingale sings in the woods alone
And who taketh note of the other birds:
The glades being thrilled by her glorious bars
Piped through the leaves when the round pure moon
Has arisen, chasing the sparkling stars.

MADONNA.

A COUNTRY chancel overseas,
  A gentle girl is kneeling there,
  Her fair hands clasped in fervent prayer,
Her dark locks ruffled by the breeze
  That comes in at the open door
  With cool fresh scents of mead and shore.

A clear soul this still sabbath eve
  Swayed upward unto the high light,
  Where dwell the hosts of those in white,
In joy that no man may conceive;
  A pure soul pleading there for me,
  Afar from her beyond the sea.

A tone that peals amid the swell
  Of rustic voices mingling praise
  Of Him who makes the summer days
Of sweet-breathed hours delectable.
  At close, an instant's upward glance
  Meeting the Master's in a trance.

Bowed in the twilight finally
  The dear saint face, the soft hands prest,
  The violets clustered on her breast
Shaken with one last prayer for me ;
  Though I, alack, am wild and rough,
  ˙And merit little of her love.

LOVE LETTER.

The evening skies are lightened,
   The thunderclouds are gone;
The air is cooled and brightened
   By shower and by sun;
And in this season clearest
   My cares are shaken off,
While writing to my dearest
   A letter, full of love.

O Sadness, come to-morrow,
   But leave me for to-day;
O drooping, tearful Sorrow,
   Your hour has passed away,
And narrow selfish blindness
   For this while be forgot;
Yea, all the world's unkindness
   This hour can touch me not.

LOVE LETTER.

But sweetest influences
   Be round me as I write,
And bathe my sober senses
   In dreams of deep delight:
That—as in golden armour—
   My spirit may be seen
To take its way to charm her
   Whom I have crowned my queen.

O Muse! whose mouth rehearses
   Upon thy Helicon
All honey-sweet love-verses
   That make melodious moan:
Verse-gracer! deign to grace mine
   With lucky chosen words
That shall breathe a scent of jasmine,
   And speak like singing-birds.

Then, thou fair-fashioned letter,
   Fly far, and find my dear;
But, O, be sure to meet her
   When nobody is near—
That her sweet lips be hasted
   Kisses on thee to lay:
A bliss I have not tasted,
   This many, many a day.

Ah! guide her sweet thoughts thither,
    Where, in fair flowery spots,
We bound our lives together
    With blue forget-me-nots;
There tell her that I wander
    In thought, to tryst with her,
And see the woodland squander
    Much wealth of wildflower.

Bright bluebells fill the hollow,
    White stitchwort drapes the slope;
Never was mead more yellow
    With May-bred buttercup
Than is one mossy level,
    Deep hid in the green gloom,
With the sweetest growth of April:
    The cowslip's golden plume.

There, where the boughs drooped round her
    To touch her shoulders fine,
Remind her how I found her,
    And took her hands in mine,
And told her how I loved her,
    Though she had said me nay—
Until at last I moved her,
    And chased her frowns away,

LOVE LETTER.

And took her kiss-closed promise
    To love me evermore—
Until the day fail from us,
    Upon Death's lonely shore—
Although she blushed thereafter,
    Yet smiled amid her pride ;
So tearful—in her laughter,
    And happy—when she sighed.

In primrose-paven places
    The pleasant blackbird calls,
Along the verdured passes
    Through flower-crowded knolls ;
And the soft tide of glad branches
    Sweet-ripples overhead,
Where we two have walked with fancies
    Too joyful to be said.

Ah ! there my spirit lingers
    To taste the springtime's charm,
To draw her slender fingers
    Lightly along my arm ;
And tenderly down-glancing,
    To meet her lifted gaze :
Timid, but heart-entrancing
    Beyond a poet's praise.

K

Yea, letter, thou shalt deem her,
   As I do—blossom-sweet;
Yet, O, pray her remember
   My love, until we meet:
Lest she should hate thee, letter,
   Or time have changed her mind
To tear my words, and scatter
   Thy fragments to the wind.

Nay, nay! she loves me truly,
   Her maiden heart is set;
The vows we plighted duly
   She never can forget;
And she will know my writing,
   And press it to her heart,
And read it o'er, delighting,
   Alone and far apart.

Yes, letter, on thy cover
   My love shall kiss her name,
And, thinking of her lover,
   Shall flush with joyful shame;
And I will kiss you, letter,
   Before I let you go:
And so my lips will greet her,
   And nobody will know.

LOVE LETTER.

Yea, all this while I miss her
    With exquisite, sweet pain,
Until I shall re-kiss her
    And clasp her shape again,
O my verses—be her lover
    And kiss her day by day,
And she will repeat you over
    When I am far away.

DEAD LEAVES.

The flowers you gave me are faded, friend;
   The flowers you gave me are faded.
May-time surely must come to an end,
And its garlands wither and ravel and rend;
The richest sunset its gold will spend,
   And heaven and earth be shaded.

No summer is too soon over, girl;
   No summer is too soon over:
Weary we grow of the mellow merle,
And the far-away cloud's unfruitful curl;
The joys of the morn at eve are sterile.
   A lover must be a rover.

DISILLUSION.

> "Say a day without the ever."
> *As You Like It.*

Your proud eyes give me their wearied splendour;
   Your cold loose touch, and your colder smile,
The truth to my jealous heart surrender :—
   You tire, having loved me a little while.
Ah! well, my sweet, I was sure you would,
   For I knew you false when I saw you fair.
I have watched and watched for your altered mood,
   And have schooled me so that I shall not care.

The knoll's blue bonnet, the dell's green mantle,
   The mid-wood hollow where waters run,
The bare, stained shore, with its white surf-sandal,
   The sudden smile of the gallant sun—
Will change not, be you or sweet or bitter :
   A heart after all is hard to break;
But the world at sweetest were surely sweeter
   If only sweet for your own sweet sake.

Yea, I know right well, if our love were sterling
   We had drained the earth and the skies of joy;
But I—God wot!—and you too, my darling,—
   No rare fair flower of girl and boy :
How should we rise to such exaltation
   As climbs from a cloud a splendid star?
How live—how love with such perfect passion,
   We—who are only what others are?

DOLLS.

A CHILDISH verse of a far-off May.
Basking in beauty the landscape lay :
The lingering violets were few,
But speedwell speckled the bank with blue ;
And clover was blossoming here and there,
And scented with lilac was the air ;
And cowslips were deep and rich of tint,
And the tender meadowsweets white as lint ;
And the bee hummed merrily over the mead,
And the mavis piped like Apollo's reed.
 From the light bright showers that had passed away
Shone all the freshlier earth's array :
From topmost tuft to lowliest blade
The growths were gladdened and greener made,
And leaf and bough, and bud and bush,
And twig and blossom and thicket and rush
Were tender and fragrant, moist and lush,

In the warm rich light of the glowing ray.
   Then you ran with your doll through our orchard,
    May,
And I fell to laughing as I were mad
(Such joyaunce then as a child I had)—
Laughed aloud in excess of glee,
And you fell a-laughing along with me,
But low, May, low—as your wont was aye,—
Merrily, May, but low—low.
And I remember, laughing so,
I took you, May, by your childish waist
In my childish arm, and your sweetness placed
On the seat between the beech and the lime ;
And we laughed there together a merry time.
I was eager to tell you a merry jest
And could not for laughter merriest,
For laughing, for laughing, O May, May.
I put my hand round your little neck,
Laughing as though my heart would break ;
And your little hand on my shoulder lay,
Drawing me closer, May, May,
Laughing so neither a word could say.
I put my face far into your hair,
So crisp and curly, glossy and black
(I wish I had never drawn it back) ;
I laid my throat on your shoulder fair,
Laughing, laughing, O May, May ;

Laughing I strove to speak in your ear,.
While you were laughing, O May, in mine ;
Naught of the tale myself could hear ;
Naught of it, May, could you divine.

That garden of youth is black with a curse
Which has withered the flower and frozen the bird.
We are older now ; and we put by the verse
With a tear suppressed, and a sneer—How absurd !

YEAR'S END.

The sky is dark and rainy,
  Low-arched with wheeling cloud;
The fields are steeped and fenny,
  The wind is swift and loud;
And barren boughs are shaken,
  And withered leaves are whirled
Through night—of stars forsaken,
  The pall of a dead world.

Now is December dying
  By pale and dreary chills,
With weary, weary crying
  Upon the wretched hills.
'Tis growing late and later,
  The dawning draweth nigh;
And revellers must scatter,
  And lovers bid good-bye.

YEAR'S END.

And we—'twere well to sever
    Before the daylight break.
You know it is for ever,
    This parting that we make.
Some time you may regret me
    And wonder if I live,
But if you can—forget me,
    And if you can—forgive.

I found—I leave you—lonely;
    With fate we may not cope:
The march of life is only
    The funeral of Hope.
How wise the heart that suffers
    Until the story ends,
With a kiss for its light lovers,
    And a smile for its false friends.

Not warned that faith is roving
    And happy fortune crossed,
We on the cards of loving
    Have staked our all—and lost.
Henceforth we bear our burden
    With guilty, Cain-like heart,
And only this for guerdon—
    To take our ways apart.

And all this place of bowers
  And alleys vaulted o'er,
Once blissful—once called ours—
  We flee for evermore;
The rain may rot and wreck it,
  Though as a dream 'twas fair;
The wind may sweep it naked,
  But we shall never care.

THE LAST TRYSTING.

O LOVE, thy cheeks are chill and pale
    As on the meads the early mist,
Thy tender face and fingers frail
    The bleak air hath unkindly kissed,
Thy loose dark tresses gleam with dew
Shed over thy sweet shoulders too.

Love, are we met to say farewell?
    In this wood's promise-hallowed halls
Shall these pure lips prove infidel,
    Forswearing their true faith as false?
Or is the passing weakness o'er?—
Are we true lovers as before?

Look up, thine eyes are very fair;
    Look up, love; let me read my lot.
The warm tears break through hands and hair
    Clasped closely;—thou repliest not.
Thou still art mine, these bright tears say.
Alas! thou wavest me away.

Shake hands. We shall not meet again;
    It is for ever that we part.
Good-bye! No bitter words of pain
    Shall mock what heart would say to heart.
But all the saddened heaven will moan
For grief to think what thou hast done.

LEAVE-TAKING.

The paths of our lives are parted here;
   Our feet fare ever asunder now,
As breaks the landscape, sharp and sheer,
   Slope from slope, at this breezy brow:
With on either side a wood and a stream,
And a town far down in the distance dim,
With domes that hover, with spires that gleam,
   And swimming vapours that climb and bow.

Look you, we stand on the open down
   In the empty tent of the open sky;
I can speak with you here between blue and brown,
   To stonechat's twitter and lapwing's cry.
Or ever we turn for ever apart
I can say my say to you heart to heart;
I shall not shrink and you need not start:
   We are not lovers now—you and I.

That is agreed since you will it so,
  But we meet here by chance with none beside :
Meet as we used to do long ago,
  But shall never again, whate'er betide.
For now indeed I am not your lover,
Though your face be the fairest mine eyes discover ;
Graves are between us, we step not over,
  But turn from each other.   The world is wide.

And one goes eastward, and one goes westward ;
  One into glory that gilds much gloom,
And one has no more of worstward or bestward,
  But takes the duties and days as they come.
And, parting, we think upon settled faces
That sleep in peace, while the sad cloud chases
The peeping sun from the dewy daisies
  And rude winds ruffle the salt sea foam.

O God, O God, that it should be so :
  The hoarse vast grave in the sea-field sterile,
And the pained wild eyes, and the broken, slow,
  Changed utterance eased in the fever's peril.
O, Death brings the noble a noble rest
In the chill sea's depth and the earth's chill breast ;
'Tis the grave in the heart that is gloomiest,
  Where souls rot, murdered in deadly quarrel.

I loved you truly, and palm to palm
   I tell you so, meeting your proud wet eye.
See, my tears are done, and my sobs are calm,
   Our lovings are over eternally ;
If the dead arise, I shall know, perchance,
Your adored pure forehead, your clear sweet glance—
And adore as I used, and your soul entrance
   To love as I loved you.   Till then good-bye.

A LATE PASSER.

*"There is one hope too like despair
For prudence to smother."*
                                    SHELLEY.

Down the stormy stream,
  Down the stream to the sea.
Broken—lost like a dream,
  All that was dear to me.
Would God my work in the world were done,
And I forgotten and dead and gone.

Plunge of the water beneath
  As of a soul to its doom;
Weary, aweary am I of breath,
  Ah! for the rest of the tomb.
The pine leans over the raging river,
So my heart longs to be still for ever.

Hangs not the parapet clear
  O'er the darkness that gurgles below?
Ah! to blot out year upon year
  In the black pool's eddying flow.
But I would not be false for the ease of the dead,
What hides the Future that I can dread?

Have I any hope—any faith?
　　Have I anything left to lose?—
Have I any trust but in Death,
　　Waited for—ah! God knows!
For Death is as God in mercy and might,
And shall not the Judge of the earth do right?

Down the stormy stream,
　　Out on the infinite sea.
Deep sleep after this feverish dream,
　　With all that is dear to me.
So dying hourly, drag on.　Be brave,
It cannot be very far to the grave.

PIANO-EASEL.

" Not so young as to love a woman for singing."
King Lear.

Over the white and over the black,
   Over the ebon and ivory keys,
Your fingers dance in a wild bright rack
   Of gleefully eddying melodies;
Your laugh rings clear and your curls toss free,
But the mirth and the music are not for me.

And I chafe not, lacking so slight a boon:
   Having lost all heart in the days gone by
To a brighter girl and a blither tune,
   Delight making dizzy both ear and eye;
Wherefore let laughter and curls float free,
Your mirth and your music are not for me.

MAVOURNEEN.

I THINK she knew I loved her,
   I think she knew it well;
And knew it as a secret
   Too exquisite to tell;
That time I walked beside her
   Beneath the branches boon,
In sunshine of the joining
   Of eve and afternoon.

For there are ways of speaking
   More eloquent than words:
Beside us flowed the streamlet,
   Around us piped the birds.
We spoke not of betrothal,
   I claimed of her no kiss;
But cold, and sweet, and splendid,
   She knew she gave me bliss.

We knew the future doubtful,
    But we knew the present sweet:
She knew my soul was lying
    In heaven at her feet;
But proud, and pure, and noble,
    Her eyes and forehead said
That stately heights of passion
    A stately soul should tread.

I loved her grace and frankness,
    Her glance's bluebell light;
I loved the daisy petal
    Of her cheek's pure red and white;
I loved her for the beauty
    Of her maidenhood and youth.
But most I loved the coldness
    Of her courage and her truth.

O gallant master-moment
    When our eyes—unshrinking—met,
And she gave me of the speedwell
    With her bosom mignonette!
I swear by that she loved me,
    With a love too great and brave
To let me sink beneath her,
    Unworthy passion's slave.

—Ah ! sly coquettish sirens,
　　You lose by Cupid's arts ;
Lose—in this game of living
　　To cheat for broken hearts ;
Lose—by your cloyed temptations
　　Of traitorous smiles and sighs ;
Love is an athlete archer
　　With aweless artist eyes.

Yet each after his fashion
　　May think of love and life :
The week-day humdrum honey
　　Of the husband and the wife,
And the raving melodrama
　　Of the dagger and the bowl.
Enough for me to live and love
　　With brain, and heart, and soul !

SONG.

When fields were green and skies were clear
   And bluebells paved the woods of Spring,
I weighed the world against her tear,
   And found her tear the dearer thing.

But while I followed gain and fame,
   And in the great world played my part,
I changed;—but she remained the same:
   And now I think it broke her heart.

NOT AS YOU LIKE IT.

In a showery Irish August
   Of mild bright sun and wind
They met in the Wicklow valleys—
   Orlando and Rosalind.

And glorious was valley and valley,
   And splendid was height and height;
And she was a budding maiden,
   And he was a woodland knight.

And the ether was so transparent,
   And so fresh the azure sheen,
And the colour so pure and perfect
   Of bluff and velvet ravine—

All purple and silver and emerald
   Set deeply in golden mirth,
With the clouds overstraying like angels
   Coming down to behold the earth;

And so priceless the fame of their fathers
   Received in those crystal hours,
That the young hearts budded and blossomed
   And kissed like sister flowers;

Not thinking of death or exile
   Or the daily part to play,
But only the sweet of the season
   When life makes holiday.

And Orlando proffered his princess
   The life to her father due,
And the chain that was warm from her bosom
   O'er his bended neck she threw.

For he knelt at her feet victorious
   And blameless beyond rebuke;
And her hand stayed not from rewarding,
   And her voice as she thanked him shook:

Till his loyalty chilled and trembled
   At the tender tremulous tone,
At the clasp of the clinging fingers,
   And the eyes that hung on his own;

At the innocence of her maidhood,
   At the trust of her noble youth,
At the generous eighteen Aprils
   That shone in her guileless growth.

NOT AS YOU LIKE IT.

And his glorying died in his pity,
  And his beautiful pride was marred,
At the dignified childish richness
  Giving all itself for reward.

O, if all himself could have matched it
  And given her worth for worth,
He had kissed her there and had grappled
  In wrestle with all the earth.

But the soul springs not with the shoulder,
  And hands tear never apart
The coils of cold chain-cable
  That sink round a buried heart.

For he thought of his desperate portion,
  And his home jarred past redress;
And he thought as he looked on the maiden
  Of his own unworthiness:

And he loved her better, O! better,
  Than to spring to her vermeil mouth,
And quaff the wild torrent of kisses
  That trembled in flood for his drouth;

And he turned from the blue eyes brimming,
  And the young cheeks burning beneath,
As a soldier who turns to his duty
  Albeit the duty be death.

And she kept back her tears' hot gushing,
    And she held up her princely brow,
And she took his soul as he gave it
    In his parting glance and bow.

And I know not if care or trouble
    Befell in Arden immense,
But a tumult of rain and lightning
    Passed over the Wicklow glens.

A ROMANCE REOPENED.

It had rained on the wharves and chimneys
    And the air was clean and cool,
As I walked on the terminus platform
    In the city of Liverpool;

O the grace of that sabbath evening,
    O the charm of my true love's land,
And the spring of my statured spirit
    As at touch of my true love's hand.

And by me the passenger engine
    Slid up, while its giant breath
Caught all my soul from my keeping
    In a battle of life and death:

I stood in a dream on the planking,
    By a terrible hope dismayed;
In a glow of tremendous daring
    That almost made me afraid:

For I saw, past the passenger engine,
    Lost angel-fair true-lover smiles;
And I muttered, "From here to my heaven
    Is hardly a hundred miles,—

"One rush with this greyhound-outrunner,
    One outbreak of passion long foiled,
And the years of my grieving are ended
    And the spoilers of youth are despoiled."

And two men parted beside me,
    Shaking hands at the carriage door,
Saying, "Good-bye, brother, I love her
    For ever and evermore."

O my own little ringleted darling!
    O her eyelashes, heavily wet,
As she kissed me, and clung on my shoulder
    That last last time that we met.

O, I love her; I perish without her,
    Though I stun me with pleasure and care:
My mirth and my profit are hollow,
    The masks of a ghastly despair.

O delusion of yesterday's pleasure,
    O dulness of yesterday's pain,
Behold how I toss you with curses
    To the wheels of the out-springing train.

Lo, an iron knee on my bosom,
    An iron hand at my throat,
And the might of the monster engine
    Flung back to some place remote;

And the still small voice of duty,
  More harsh than an engine could,
Hissing hard in my ear, "You promised,
  And you know it was *right* you should :

"For you draw on her young head curses,
  That smite like a vengeful sword,
And you warp her from honour and duty
  And the faith of a plighted word."

So my soul fell down in its torment
  And weltered and wailed in despair,
While the damps of ineffable anguish
  Were clustered and cooled in my hair.

"O," I cried, "she is pure as the rosebud
  That showers and summershine swell ;
Shall I smite her with plague of my passion,
  Who loves me but too too well ?

"I have promised to fly from her presence,
  And trample my wildness and greed,
Nor set in her pathway and pillow
  The thorn of a mutinous deed ;

"But shall I not see her nor hear her,
  Nor learn if she suffer or thrive ?
Not——Ah ! God—do I know since long long ago
  Even if she be dead or alive ?

" But one gaze in her eyes' young lustres,
   One story of suffering to tell:
And she springs to my side a pitying bride—
   Springs, ah! from heaven to hell.

" Black engine, you swallow-outflyer,
   You are speedy and fearful and strong,
Will you mangle the hearts of the sinless,
   And rush in the service of Wrong?

"You are glutted with rivers of water
   And mountains on mountains of coal,
Is your burning fiery furnace
   Yet agape for a human soul?

"O, 'tis truly I love her, God help me!
   I will bear for her truly and well,
Let her bide in the peace of her pureness
   Though for me be the fire-pits of hell."

So my soul, in the dust and ashes,
   Knelt down to its burthen of care;
And methought that her far away kisses
   Burnt blessing and pain on my hair.

And the young heart died in my bosom,
   And the young blood failed from my cheek,
But before me the devil-engine
   Went out, with a piercing shriek.

UNDER THE GILDING.

We were at a wedding breakfast met,
   Where beauty was bought by a Christian Jew,
And merchant and matron and miss were set,
   And actor and artist and scribbler too,

And priests who had blessed the bridal twain—
   Pah ! such a union of maid and man !
There was never such boredom of bright champagne
   And tawdry talk since the world began.

I was there to harden myself in shame
   Against high illusions long overpast :
I had years twenty-five when that morning came,
   And illusions rarely till twenty last.

I was skilled, I thought, in the wise world's ways ;
   But the practised jest on my lips was dumb :
I was sick of my partner's bridemaid-face,
   And I poisoned with loathing the healths to come.

They prated around me I knew not what—
    Of some woman who was—or was not—fair
And kind and true ; till my face grew hot
    And my eyes turned stone in a tortured stare,

And I felt my joints grown deadly stiff,
    And my sense all jarred with a guilty start ;
So that scarcely I gasped my breath, as if
    At a red-hot grasp on my naked heart.

For I knew the lady they chattered of,
    And her peerless beauty of pitiless frost :—
The cruel queen of my wild first love,
    Whom I worshipped for seven years—and lost.

HER WINDOW.

> "The angel woman-faces we have seen,
> And angel woman-spirits we have guessed."
> CLOUGH.

My one star in heaven—her window,
　My one goal on earth—her breast;
And my dreamed-of sinless Eden—
　This room of her maiden rest.

Here the moonlight and sunrise kissed her
　As she dreamed—on the flower-like mouth
And august sweet eyes that created
　And slew the soul of my youth.

It was here that she prayed and slumbered,
　And loosed and upwound her hair:
And fostered the matchless beauty
　That pierced me of old with despair.

It was here that her long-dead mother
   Set the place of her curtained bed,
Where she veiled the growth of her glory
   Till the morn she went to be wed.

And now the high shrine of my worship
   Stands desolate, bleak, and strange;
And my first love and I drift sundered,
   On the graveward currents of change.

It is long since I passed by her garden
   Where I failed not in days of old;
It is long since the light of her glamour
   Has died into gloom from gold.

So that here as I carelessly wander,
   'Twixt a smile and a sigh I start
To find of her memory remaining
   But the scar of her step on my heart.

The workmen are smoking and jesting,
   With their ladders and pots of paint,
In the innermost bower of my angel,
   The sanctuary of my saint.

And I stride, scarce abashed, through the litter
   To the goal of my yearnings of yore;
And I kneel not or bow in the temple
   I had once given eternity for.

So the stricken stands now as a spoiler,
　Beholding her glory brought low,
And profanes her high throne, and the stately
　Cold splendour that wounded me so.

And yet—nay; for nobly I loved her,
　Mere statue of ice though she were.
And I give her but thanks for her mission
　To teach to my eyes what was fair,

Though indeed she would turn from my coffin
　In beauty unaltered, and say—
" The singer who loved and forgot me
　Is now only festering clay."

I think of her but as a vision
　That brought to me heavenly gleams,
As a cloud or a face or a poem
　Brings transient heavenly dreams.

The cloud is a mist in the sunshine;
　The poem a blossom of Art;
Our goddess, an exquisite image,
　Celestial—except at the heart.

And God makes these coreless fair women,
　And bright clouds that pass as we gaze,
To mock us—it may be—a little,
　Yet rouse us to follow His ways.

God sends them to teach us and spur us
  To aspire far beyond and above :
The creature, the cloud—are illusions;
  The certainties—worship and love.

Love !—Ah, for the dream of my boyhood !—
  For the Good of our life-long quest !—
Is *it* even as the dust and defilement
  In this room of my first love's rest?

LEUCONOË.

O FIRM be my pulse, and my hot brain cool,
   And my heart as 'tis ever wont to be;
For when saw I aught more beautiful
   Than her cheeks and eyes as she walks with me?

Under the skies of this fairy clime,
   In the dawn of triumphant womanhood,
Straying with me in a fairy time,
   By fairy city, and stream, and wood.

Park, and garden, and avenue,
   And palace and fane, and spires and towers,
And skies of mother-of-pearl and blue,
   Odours of June—and all this ours.

Pinnacled stateliness, pastoral grace,
   And foliaged vistas blocked with bloom,
And tides of crystal that interlace,
   About thicket and lawn, and in light and gloom,

While beds of the blissful forget-me-not
    In river, and glade, and garden rise—
To look at their tender colouring, caught
    In the modest irids of her young eyes.

And red may and guelder mix overhead,
    As to match her cheek's ethereal tint;
And chestnut blossom is heavily shed
    For her carpet—in faint pink snows without stint.

She, in perfect, virginal sovereignty,
    So carelessly candid, and sweet in her part;
And I, with such brands and blights on me,
    Here at her side, with a fluttering heart:

Though Life I have found such a mangling snare,
    And the grave so greedy of noble youth;
Though wrinkled and wasted am I with care,
    And haggard with quest of the mirage—Truth.

I!—awaked from unrest, among blossoming trees
    Of this English scene, for a delicate space,
To the charm and spell of Ovocan peace
    In the sensitive calm of her mind and face!

No statue—that knows but its spell-bound slave,
    And slays him calmly and cruelly
With scorn as cold as the moss on a grave—
    Is the glowing true woman who walks by me;

No trustfully helpless, tender child,
  In a blind, great, fervid passion of love
Caught along, like a plume in a tempest wild,
  Into heartbreak and death, amid surges rough;—

But I know her brain as I know my own,
  And the trained rare force of her intellect,
Unique in woman—and void alone
  Of the knowledge the harmless and sweet reject.

So I could not deceive her—even if I would:
  She is queen over passion, and queen over scorn;
Benign in the strength of her womanhood;
  Open-eyed, pure as the breaking morn.

And I—sworn lieger of Intellect
  And the Will to choose Right, and the Sense of
    Grace—
By her in these shades that the tides reflect,
  Enthralled by her voice, looking down on her face.

We know each other as equal and friend:
  She would not be my queen; I would not be
    her lord.
But I would we were lovers till our lives' end—
  One in heart and work, and in aim and hoard.

But I cannot play with her as one plays
   In brainless jest with a ball-room belle,
To divine what her heart would grant of grace
   To me as a lover.—Ah! well, well,

Let me rest, and but the pure blossom cull
   Of the moment here under the greenwood tree;
For when saw I aught more beautiful
   Than her cheeks and eyes as she walks with me?

A WINTER NIGHT.

The saying is the serpent's,
  But I take it at the odds :
Did ye know good and evil
  Then ye should be as gods.

O fair must be the heaven
  That opes beyond the grave,
If it be like the heaven
  Spread over field and wave.

And sweet must be the future
  In bright Elysian fields,
If it excel the beauty
  And joy the Present yields.

To live the life God gives us,
  With blessed pleasures rife,
Is— sure ! the way to thank Him
  For Everlasting Life.

Did sweet Miss Mahon dream it
  This evening, as we drove
Under the wintry crescent
  Along the wintry grove?

Dream of the ecstatic stillness
  Of eve on mead and mere?
Dream how divine our breathing
  The natural atmosphere?

Dream how supremely lovely
  Her face and figure were:
The noble classic figure,
  The classic weight of hair?

Dream how divine the kindling
  Of health in eye and cheek?
Dream how divine the smiling
  She wore to hear me speak?

Dream how inspired her graveness
  When we let all speech die
Under the holy silence
  Of universal sky?

Dream of the wayside runnel,
  A wheel-crashed icy bar?
Dream that she shone in woman
  My loftiest crystal star?

A WINTER NIGHT.

Dream of her queenly, careless,
  Mild bliss of pure content,
As under elfin branches
  In elfin light we went?

Ah! does she dream I ponder
  Here—hours on hours—alone,
The charm of being with her,—
  Her every look and tone?

Ah! does she dream what fills me,
  Making dull slumber flee,
To think that she reposes
  Under one roof with me?

Ah! were I sure she dreamed it
  And shared my trance of bliss,
The future could do nothing
  But cloy or copy this.

A FROSTFERN.

I DREAMED last night of you, dearest,
    As the stars in their courses went
Over all this gleam and chiming
    Of the streams and spires of Ghent;
I dreamed of your blushing pureness
    Through the hours of the world's eclipse,
And awoke with the consecration
    Of your innocent kiss on my lips.

It was only deceitful fancy
    That played such a flattering part,
For how could I hope to tenant
    The shrine of your angel-heart?
But the thought of your fairy presence,
    And the taste of your visioned kiss,
Have illumined a winter waking
    With an April of laughing bliss.

GLADIATRIX.

Face to face once more we stand,
And you proffer me your hand,
    And your eyelashes gleam wet,
    As you ask me to forget
    What took place when last we met.

I can not forget while living,
But I grant you my forgiving
    For your stabs of long ago.
    When I loved your sister so,
    Why were you my deadly foe?

Though I feel you evil throughly,
How can I abhor you duly
    While you yet such likeness bear
    To my darling's eyes and hair,
    And her sensitive sweet air?

Her intoxicating smile
Masks your soul's consummate guile;
    And her low voice you have still—
    Strange! the puzzle of the will,
    Hers to suffer—yours to kill.

Kill ! although she loved you well.
Ah ! the old insatiate spell
    Quickens into life apace
    With the beauty of your race
    On your statuesque pale face

And serene supernal brow:
Beaming calmly on me now,
    As the last taunt to be borne
    Of your avalanche of scorn
    Hurled on me that far-off morn

When you found her at my side
All but pledged to be my bride,
    And your traitorous gracious art
    Rent our knitted lives apart
    By the vow that broke her heart.

*   *   *   *   *

Vilest devil in her shape,
I can curse you, and escape
    From the hell you lure me to :
    O, till now I never knew
    That you loved me—loved me—*you !*

LADY BLANCHE'S AUSTRALIAN.

> "There are things of which I may not speak;
> There are dreams that cannot die;
> There are thoughts that make the strong heart weak;
> And bring a pallor into the cheek,
> And a mist before the eye."
> LONGFELLOW.

HE sprawled on a couch and watched the rinkers,
   The tawny Australian millionaire:
Tawny his gold-digging gold-crusted fingers,
   And tawny as gold his beard and hair.
And the Lady Blanche's imperial grace,
Because she had known him in younger days,
   And because she was sweet as sweet could be,
     And because he was bored by her Guardsman friend
   About his colonial cavalry—
Approached, through the crowd of London fashion,
In all the splendour of beauty and station;
   And smiled, and spoke at the sofa-end.

The capitalist in comforters
Was enthralled by that soft sweet voice of hers :
They sat them down on the velvet fine,
The Highland pipes playing "Auld Lang Syne."

" You remember the summer my father died,
And my home set sail for the world's other side.—
   Well, yes; my lady. 'Twas as you say.—
   But I remember as yesterday,
Meeting you later—in rain and wind—
   Near our county town by the hills and bay;
For I found an excuse to linger behind,
   In a tender dream that haunts me yet;—
   And then I tore myself wholly away.
Stayed over the space of half a year,
To breathe your belovèd atmosphere.—
   Do you remember when last we met?

" What splendid surprise in your noble eyes!
   Be at ease. My wife and my boys are here;
   And my brain is as cool as the gem in your ear.

" But—do you remember? The sky was grey,
   And the streets were still, and the ground dry-white;
And I, in the sweet of the crystal day,
   Walked, and mused of my lost delight :—

Your pale cheek, pure as the autumn air—
　The stateliness of your gentle eyes—
The thundercloud of abundant hair—
　The lips that closed in lovelier wise
Than any others.　My sweet white girl!
　The window set in my life's dark chamber,
　To give me the sunshine's molten amber,
And silver floods of the air's pure pearl,
　And cool fresh breath of morn and even,
　And all the joy of the open heaven.

—" Why should I tell you a dismal story—
The wretched wreck of a young life's glory—
How love and content were smitten together
With all the sweetness of Northern weather?

" I turned my face from the taints of town
To breathe myself on the lonely down,
And I said, ' I will take the path by the river,
Though at the Yule-tide the boughs bud never,
Yet grandly o'erhead swings the bare dark branch;'—
And behold you were there before me, Blanche!

" Do you remember?　You walked alone,
　By the rustling reeds of the river shore,
And a wind arose—till your veil was blown
　From the fluttering cluster of plumes you wore;

And you saw as you turned from the stinging blast,
How I reached for your veil as it flitted past,
And tracked it, and caught it, and clasped it fast.

" A shade came over the shuddering world.
   Uprose the voice of the wildernesses,
     The great gust roared in the high tree-tops,
     And smote down before it the leafless copse;
   The river moaned in its black recesses;
The long boughs over us lashed and whirled;
   And the placid pools were alive with dancers,
   As the sleet came down like a charge of lancers.

" You came to me down the darkened path,
Rapt in a ravin of winter's wrath,
In the stunning stroke and the flaying breath—
Hurled, like a berry that withereth,
Almost from my outstretched hands as you caught
   them—
Lifted and whirled like a leaf of autumn.

" Do you remember, my storm-tossed dove?
It was over a mile to a human roof,
   Through the ravaging wind and raging rain;
But I hid your beauty from rude reproof,
   Though the hurricane struck at you might and main.

Ah! you smile—with a blush and a tear—to remember
  What I shall forget not while I live,—
Your making with me such a mad-brained clamber
  Up to the cleft of the leaning cliff:
How I kept your skirts from the draggled ferns,
And tore your curls from the grasp of the thorns;
  How we crossed the breach in the rock-crashed
      hedge,
  And stepped the plashes from edge to edge
  On faggots flung in the spongy sedge.
And so—On—Up. Till you laughed at last,
With the dark pine ranks about you massed,
At the stabbing storm as it galloped past.

—"Friends who have parted, ah! so widely,
Here once more, joining the right hands gladly;
Tasting anew the sweet old savour,
Through all the strangeness of foreign favour!—

" Even then our lives had turned asunder :—
  One, whole and pure as an opening flower,
The other, marked by the marring thunder,
  Standing : a lonely broken tower.—
And we gossiped of past and coming changes,
Of friends whom distance and time estranges—
  Differing gleanings of girl and boy :—
Your wild hair blown into tangled eddies,
  To give your comb, as you said, employ;

And beyond all loveliness of all ladies
   That the fates to my roving eyes disclose,—
   Your cheeks,—rain-kissed into lilied rose.

"Well, time from all idols our fancy weans,
   But I remember you as in your teens.
Do you remember?—Among your daughters
   Such talk from a stranger comes in with a wrench.
But you know now a thing which many waters,
   As saith the Scripture, can *never* quench."

He stood up to meet his young Australians;
And Guardsmen beaux, looking small by those aliens,
Brought Lady Blanche's girls to their mother.
The young people haughtily bowed to each other;
But Lady Blanche's gloved braceleted hand,
   With a mournful smile of refulgent calm,
Was given those lads of Omana-land
   And crushed in the gold-digger's horny palm.

So they met and parted,—there at the rink;
And their hearts were lifted and filled, I think,
With sense of what Life—and its dreams—must
   mean,
As the band struck into—"God save the Queen!"

VIGNETTES.

IN THE ENGINE SHED.

The air was heavy with greasy vapour;
  The walls were like cinders; the floor, of slack.
The engine-driver came to his labour,
  A good-humoured corpulent old coal-sack,
With a thick gold chain where it bulged the most,
And a beard like a brush, and a face like a toast,
And a hat half-eaten by fire and frost;
And a diamond pin in the folded dirt
Of the shawl that served him for collar and shirt
  Whenever he harnessed his steed of mettle :—
The shovel-fed monster that could not tire,
With limbs of steel and entrails of fire;
  Above us it sang like a big tea-kettle.

  Now, I wouldn't have him think I'd note it,
Much less—ever dream that I wrote it,
. But he came to his salamander toils
  In one of the Devil's cast-off suits,
All charred, and discoloured with rain and oils
  And smeared and sooted from muffler to boots.

Some wiping—it struck him—his paws might suffer
With a wisp of threads he found on the buffer;
(The improvement indeed was not very great).
Then he spat, and passed his pipe to his mate.

And his whole face laughed with an honest mirth,
As any extant on this grimy earth,
   Welcoming me to his murky region;
And had you known him, I tell you this—
Though your bright hair shiver and shrink at its roots
   O piano-fingering fellow-collegian—
You would have returned no cold salutes
To the cheery greeting of hearty Chris,
But ungloved your hand, and locked it in his.

   The icy sleet-storm shatters and scatters,
And falls on the pane like a pile of fetters;
He flies through it all with the world's love-letters:
The master of mighty leviathan-motions
   That make for him storm when the nights are fair,
   And cook him with fire and carve him with air,
While we sleep soft in the carriage cushions,
And he keeps watch on the signal red O.'s.
   Often had Chris over England rolled me;
   You shall hear a story he told me
Of tender grace and the dewy meadows.

The Story.

We were driving the down express;
   Will at the steam, I at the coal:
Over the valleys and villages,
Over the marshes and coppices,
Over the river, deep and broad;
Through the mountain, under the road,
        Flying along,
        Tearing along,
Thunderbolt engine, swift and strong,
   Fifty tons she was, whole and sole!

   I had been promoted to the express:
I warrant to me that run was gay.
It was the evening that ended May,
   And the sky—was a glory of tenderness.
We were thundering down to a midland town,—
   It doesn't matter about the name
For we didn't stop there, or anywhere
For a dozen o' miles on either side,
   So it's all the same—
             Just there you slide,
With your steam shut off, and your brakes in hand,
Down the steepest and longest grade in the land
At a pace that I promise you is grand.

We were just there with the express,
   When I caught sight of a muslin dress
On the bank ahead; and as we passed—
You have no notion of how fast—
A girl shrank back from our baleful blast.

We were going—a mile and a quarter a minute—
   With vans and carriages—down the incline!
But I saw her face, and the sunshine in it;
   I looked in her eyes, and she looked in mine
As the train went by, like a shot from a mortar:
   A roaring hell-breath of dust and smoke.
   And I mused for a minute, and then—awoke:
And she was behind us—a mile and a quarter.

And the years went on, and the express
Leaped in her black resistlessness,
Evening by evening, England through.—
   Will—God rest him !—was found—a mash
   Of bleeding rags, in a fearful smash
He made of a Christmas train at Crewe.
It chanced I was ill the night of the mess
   Or I shouldn't now be here alive;
But thereafter, the five o'clock out express,
   Evening by evening, I used to drive.

And I often saw her: that lady, I mean,
   That I spoke of before. She often stood

IN THE ENGINE SHED.

Atop of the bank ;—it was pretty high,
   Say twenty feet, and backed by a wood.—
She would pick the daisies out of the green
To fling down at us as we went by.
We had got to be friends, that girl and I,
Though I was a rugged stalwart chap,
And she a lady! I'd take off my cap
   Evening by evening, when I'd spy
That she was there, in the summer air,
   Watching the sun sink out of the sky.

Oh, I didn't see her every night :
   Bless you ! no ; just now and then,
And not at all for a twelvemonth quite.
   Then, one evening, I saw her again,
Alone as ever—but deadly pale
And down on the line, on the very rail,
While a light as of hell from our wild wheels broke,
   Tearing down the slope with their devilish clamours
   And deafening din as of giant hammers
That smote in a whirlwind of dust and smoke
   All the instant or so that we sped to meet her.
   —Never, O never, had she seemed sweeter !—
I let yell the whistle, reversing the stroke
Down that awful incline ; and signalled the guard
To put on his brakes at once, and HARD—
Though we couldn't have stopped. We tattered the rail
Into splinters and sparks, but without avail.

We couldn't stop; and she wouldn't stir,
   Saving to turn us her eyes, and stretch
   Her arms to us :—and the desperate wretch
I pitied, comprehending her.
So the brakes let off, and the steam full again,
Sprang down on the lady the terrible train.—
She never flinched. We beat her down,
And ran on through the lighted length of the town
   Before we could stop to see what was done.

   Oh, I've run over more than one !
Dozens of 'em, to be sure ; but none
That I pitied as I pitied her—
If I could have stopped—with all the spur
Of the train's weight on, and cannily—
But it wouldn't do with a lad like me
And she a lady,—or had been.—Sir ?
Who was she ?—Best say no more of her;
The world is hard. But I'm her friend,
Staunch, sir,—down to the world's end.
It's a curl of her sunny hair
Set in this locket that I wear;
I picked it off the big wheel there.—
Time's up, Jack.—Stand clear, sir. Yes,
We're going out with the express.

MIRANDA.

She stands on the ridge with her locks blown level,
  Her proud face turned to the stormy sea
And magnificent gusts—as they rise and revel,
  Whirling white spray and her fine hair free :
The rocks not more black in their drenched recesses
Than her tossing mantle of storm-dark tresses.

The thundercloud bursts in the wild rain-scourges ;
  The thunderbolt falls on the reeling hill ;
The hurricane tears up the boiling surges ;
  Her clear dark eye is untroubled still ;
For she sees not yet the brave ship of her lover,
Which even now Ariel hovers over

VESPERS.

> "But let my due feet never fail
> To walk the studious cloister's pale,
> And love the high embowèd roof,
> With antique pillars massy proof,
> And storied windows richly dight,
> Casting a dim religious light.
> There let the pealing organ blow
> To the full-voiced quire below,
> In service high, and anthems clear,
> As may with sweetness, through mine ear,
> Dissolve me into ecstasies,
> And bring all Heaven before mine eyes."
> *Il Penseroso.*

WE went at evensong, to pray
   That peace, which this world cannot give;
And duteous vows and rites to pay,
   And gather grace to rightly live.

Through meadows, filled with hawthorn scent
   And warm light from the sunken sun,
By winding flowery ways we went;
   And as the chimes were almost done,

VESPERS.

We passed in at the ivied porch
    With rustle of her silk attire,
And up along the quiet church
    To her dim alcove in the choir.

A seemly smoothing of the skirt,
    A bowing of the brow to pray;
Her meek devotion chains my heart,
    And vagrant musings pass away.

The stir adown the aisle has ceased,
    And lo! the holy sound begins
As the intoning of the priest
    Makes lamentation for our sins.

Alack, *our* sins! what sins has she
    Who kneels beside me with bent head?
Upon her tender purity,
    O righteous Lord, what taint is shed?

Our sins! Alack, this gentle girl's,
    Whose heart is meeker than a lamb's,
Whose soul is lovely as the curls
    That fall across her folded palms:

O King most Holy and most High,
    Smite not a sinner vile and mean;
How grim with clotted guilt am I
    If this white blossom be not clean!

Behold! I am too throughly base
    For her to tread on loathingly;
But for her gentleness and grace,
    May God be merciful to me.

Lo! the Magnificat swells—rich
    And solemn—from the solemn calm,
And the rapt spirit soars the pitch
    Of heaven with the sacred psalm.

And she, with bright lips—and bright eyes
    Hovering 'twixt downcast and uplift,—
Sings, like some changeling of the skies
    Strayed hither through a cloudy rift.

O King and Lord, how fair art Thou
    If this Thy creature be so fair!
Ever be it with me as now,
    Singing with angels, here or there.

Here, praising Thee a little space,
    My hushed heart listening to her;
There, praising Thee before Thy face,
    With saints—in some wise—lovelier.

Dear Lord, my cold heart is constrained
    To melt in gentle gratitude
For four fair things Thou hast ordained
    To be so gracious and so good:

VESPERS.

The spring time, and the stars, and Song,
   And smiles of Thy sweet handmaidens
That guide and cheer our steps along
   Through what were else but wastes immense.

Thy daughters, Master : purest springs
   Of all what little nobleness—
Or mere weak love of noble things—
   Has striven with the dark excess

Of evil in my wayward life :
   High thoughts they breathe, and lofty aims
In this old world, where souls grow stiff,
   And cheeks burn hard with hourly shames.

Not light loves of an idle day;
   But queens, throned in the reverent mind
Above all change or stain—to sway
   By graceful charities and kind.

How sweet the sabbath evening prayer,
   While sunset shapes its golden crown,
And fades out from the glowing air,
   As slowly God's peace deepens down :

And farther, fainter grows the bleat
   Of prosperous flocks ; and one by one
Die woodland warblings wild and sweet,
   And but the even monotone

Of pious exhortation sounds :
   While griefs, and cares, and passions lull,
What rest, and love, and bliss abounds,
   She sitting by me, beautiful.

Master, Thy child ! upon my sleeve
   See her dark ringlets !   How they shine
To bring me thankfullest belief
   In beauty, human and divine.

O Master, I am dark with guilt,
   Yet will I strive Thy grace to stir ;
Deal with me always as Thou wilt,
   But O ! deal tenderly with her.

A boon I ask, most Bountiful !—
   Not roses of her love's delight ;
Indeed I do not care to cull
   Blossoms my touch would only blight.

But, O fair Lord, upon her pour
   Thy blessing, as Thou judgest best ;
Of the full riches of Thy store
   Bestow on her the goodliest.

The preacher's words I hardly hear,
   I know their sense by heart of old ;
But their smooth flow upon my ear
   Brings to me blessings manifold.

VESPERS.

How still and peaceful all things are,
    Musing upon the things of heaven ;
High in the blue the evening star
    Is kindling, like a soul forgiven.

And all below is hushed in shade,
    Veiled in dim, hallowed, happy rest ;
While slowly, wide and wider spread
    Sweet influences, calm and blest.

Lo ! now the whispered benison,
    Descending into every heart;
God's peace be with us—every one !—
    We rise up straightway, and depart.

With HER adown the darkened aisle,
    And out into the balmy gloom,
Where the stars twinkle, clear and still,
    Through boughs that droop with heavy bloom.

PICNIC.

"Not by any means pretty,"
    The gainsaying council said
Of critics come down from the City
    To dine in the green glenhead;
For when lovers went up by the shady
    Mossed ways to the waterfall top,
We had got to discussing a lady
    With sherry and ginger-pop.

Not rich, nor clever, nor witty,
    The girl in the gipsy hat,
And—goodness gracious!—not pretty,
    There could be no doubt about that.
But then the opinions divided,
    And criticism came to a halt;
Disagreeing, deriding, derided—
    Each finding a different fault.

So I left them all squabbling together,
    These wiseacre women and men.
More sweet was the midsummer weather,
    More grand the magnificent glen ;
And strolling from crescent to crescent
    Of river that foamed from the fall,
My thoughts were none the less pleasant
    Because of Miss What-d'ye-call.

I had known the girl from a baby,
    Whose beauty had borne rebuke ;
We had blotted the self-same copy,
    And spelt from the self-same book.
And as in wild-wood bower
    Of new-grown greenery,
Opeth an April flower,—
    Even so fair was she.

WHITE ROSES.

She sat by her open piano,
   Under lavish gold of her hair,
And loosed the tide of her playing
   On the stillness of evening air:
Like a springtide surging and spreading,
   In celestial strength and grace,
From her magical floating fingers
   And the peace of her white-rose face.

Ah! what words for that saintly music,
   With divine unconsciousness played?
In a trance the starlight listened,
   And the lawns, and the laurel shade.
It was now like the roar of billows,
   With a diamond spray breaking through,
Now tenderly soft, and wondrous
   As the birth of the summer dew.

Too brief was that glimpse of heaven,
    Like an angel's visit it passed ;
Pure notes dropped, slowly and starlike,
    And she blushed—blue-eyed—at the last.
But I could remember her ever
    By that rapturous, melodied space,
By the sunset cloud of her tresses,
    And the dream on her white-rose face.

1879.

PIA.

"Puritan pansies."
E. A. Poe.

With voices hushed and heads declined
We gathered in where we had dined—
Among these pious Puritans;
And a book was brought of the hoar old man's,
And evening prayers were devoutly read;
Then straightway the good-nights were said—
While kindly hands my fingers pressed—
And weary limbs were laid to rest.
   Yet by the windows lingered I
Under the large stars of the sky,
As loth to close and put away
The volume of so sweet a day—
Last of that summer's holidays
For me, the eager toiler of town,
In the midst of my task by rail run down
For respite and rest in this blessed place.
We kept that day like a sacrament,
A mid-week sabbath of heather-scent,

Sacred and sinless from waking till now.
Along ferny valley and purple brow
And fox-gloved ravine and mossy grot
Lulled by the tinkle of trickling rills,
And at lakes far hid in the wooded hills,
Where the place praised God as our mouths could not
With waterfall thunder and sunlit rain ;
And hither we came at eve again
With maiden jesting and harmless mocks
To Ocean breaking upon his rocks.
  And now that stars were overhead,
And wise old folk were gone to bed,
Still we delayed, and would not yield
Our woodland festival fulfilled.

  Then she who was the household light,
Because it was a lovely night—
Returned, with her long hair let down
Showing the golden in the brown,
To plan with us one sally more
By the dark woods and moaning shore,
To taste the pureness of the air
That hung in dewy fragrance there.

  And I beheld with mild surprise
The exquisiteness of her eyes
Green-grey like leaves of mistletoe,
And lit with innocence and bliss ;

Her forehead smooth and high and modest,
And white round neck too highly bodiced,
And rings of hair now loose on her shawl.
   O cynical friend, you cannot know
How perfectly sweet that maiden is
From her heart to her clinging finger-tips--
With willow-like figure and rose-leaf lips—
And she never dreams she is sweet at all.
   But like as a violet blooms in the shade,
So the beauty blooms of that Puritan maid
Who stood with us there, so meekly fair,
Shame-faced—and not with braided hair,
As if on the ancient text she thought:
Nor with fine apparel richly wrought,
Nor mannered sweetness feigned with care
Her gentle image to instal
In hearts unpuritanical.
   But of lilac print was her Quaker dress,
And her soul was all maiden tenderness;
So that here she stood with her unbound tresses
Among the children who loved her well,
And spoke of the shore and the moaning swell
And the wood and the starlit lonelinesses.

   We passed out into the holy fear
Of the quiet wood-ways mossed and ferned;
And through fondling branches deeply-leaved,
We heard how the sleepless billow turned

On the pillowing sand, as the bright sea heaved.
   And coming out thus on the village pier
We saw the headland shadow the bay,
And the lighthouse twinkle from far away,
And a meteor fling out a fiery dart.
   O, deeply of peace our spirits drank
As we stood on the quay some space apart,
And the benediction of starlight sank
Over the spire and hills and woods,
And the gleaming sea's pure solitudes,
And on lips and tresses and brow and heart.

1875.

THE DREAM OF PIA.

O, THE night is weary and we are worn,
   So thorny and steep is the narrow road,
But we trust to see gleam in the golden morn
   The crystal spires of the city of God,

The jasper walls and the ivory towers,
   And the adamant gateways in lofty line;
And the River of Bliss, and the fadeless flowers,
   And the purple banner of Love Divine;

And the white-winged sentinels, helmed and girt,
   And the bugles blowing our welcome home:
We who have suffered and have not spared,
   For the hope of the promise of joys to come.

And in palace-porch and in castle-court
   The angels are glad as we enter in;
With shawms and cymbals and timbrel sport,
   They hail the children redeemed from sin.

They seal our brows with the kiss of peace,
  They bring us the stainless robe, and palm ;
They wreathe our tresses with amaranth sprays,
  Anointing with ointment, and myrrh, and balm.

And the souls we knew for our friends of yore
  Walk hand in hand with us on and on ;
Laughter and music and scent evermore
  From open window and balcony blown

Through the marble streets of the marvellous town
  Where all is wonder, where all are blest ;
Where the careful at last without thought lie down,
  Where the sick have strength, and the weary rest

On white stately terraces down to the tide
  Of the amber stream alabaster-quayed,
Reflecting high porticoes' pillared pride
  And carven trophy and balustrade.

And so we are led to the flower-strewn hall
  Where the cross is blazoned on panel and pane,
And the Lamb sits meek in the midst of them all
  For sake of whom He was foully slain ;

And the anthem rolls—as the voices throng
  Chanting together—and clear and sharp
Pulses out through the body of song
  Viol and cornet and flute and harp.

Choirs on choirs yet open up louder,
    Antiphons meet from the distances dim,
Hearts throb higher and eyes gleam prouder
    Pouring their souls in united hymn;

And ever one voice arises keen,
    A treble trilled over the praising crowd,
Until, the full strains gathering in,
    It is lost like a star in a silver cloud;

And another echoes the sweet refrain,
    Drowned in another more sweet and clear:
Echo on echo again and again,
    Throbbing and longing afar and near.

O fair Lord Christ, shall I look on Thee,
    Face to face in that glorious din;
Shall the saints about Thee make way for me,
    For me—who am sordid and foul with sin?

O Sovereign, let me but fall abashed:
    Thou hadst not once where Thy head might lie,
Though of old high anthems about Thee crashed;
    But, alas! alas! what a worm am I!—

I, who have been but Thy shame and loss,—
    I, whose exceeding iniquities nailed
Thy tender limbs to the bitter cross,
    When naught but Thy innocent blood availed!

Thou art royally gracious, and sure Thy Word
    Standeth for ever, as all shall see;
But this place too blessed Thou hast prepared,
    Too noble and lovely for one like me.

Had I died as of old Thy martyrs died,
    Torn by the brute or the fiercer flame;
Had the rack's rough crankles my joints untied,
    In eager witness of Thy loved name;

Then, haply, to-day in Thy Paradise,
    Wounded with fire or the sword or fangs,
I might undaunted behold Thine eyes,
    For Thou takest note of Thy servants' pangs.

But now, though Thy blood maketh sweet and clean,
    Is there yet of Thy ransomed so mean a one?
Wilt Thou love me, Master, and have me lean
    On Thy breast—as at supper Thy good Saint John?

Ah! meeter to fall at Thy gate and pray—
    Albeit I sully the pavement bright—
That Thou wouldst hallow me day by day
    To dwell with Thee in Thy halls of light.

And, O, be merciful. Gently deal
    With me, my flesh, and my father's house,
That we may not fail of Thy final weal,
    Or stand before Thee with shamèd brows.

EMIGRANT.

She clasped her hands on my arm;
   She laid her cheek on my shoulder;
The tide of her tears fell warm
   On hands that trembled to hold her;
I whispered a pitying word
   As the ship moved slowly apart,
And the grief of the friendless poured
   Its choking weight on my heart.

For graves in the evening shade
   Were green on a far-off hill,
Where the joys of her life were laid,
   With love that had known no chill.
But, however her heart might yearn,
   We were facing the freshening breeze;
And the white wake lengthened astern
   On the rolling floor of the seas.

She quenched the fire of her tears,
   Uplifting her meek, brave head.
"Or dark or bright be the years,
   I will take courage," she said—
Smoothing back her loose-blowing hair,
   And her shawl drawing closer the while;
So she drank in the strong sea air
   And turned away with a smile.

TO THIS BOOK.

Rein yet your pawing palfrey
   An instant ere you go;
And give me, sweet, your fingers,
   Here at your saddle bow:
Your soft ungloved brown fingers
   One instant I would press
And kiss—before you leave me,
   You dear Adventuress.

I pat your champing palfrey,
   His neck should know my hand;
Though restive and impatient,
   He will not fail to stand.
He should not reckon closely
   A minute more or less,
Now that you go for ever,
   My wild Adventuress.

TO THIS BOOK.

The bit I wrought of silver,
   Of silk I wove the rein;
I bred your foaming palfrey
   From noble-mettled strain :
It was my joy to groom him
   And braid each maney tress,
And deck him up to bear you,
   My bold Adventuress.

You chose the saddle housings,
   This girth of double strength.
My darling—and the stirrup,
   Is it of easy length?
And now too that you wear it—
   You like your riding-dress?—
Ah! dear, I think you grace it,
   You sweet Adventuress.

What friends were we in rain-time
   And happy summer sweet,
At morning and at midnight,
   In study and in street!
O, bitter were the seasons
   Of wrong and loneliness
When you were absent from me,
   You young Adventuress.

And now you kiss my forehead,
    And pray to sally forth ;
For you are proud and ardent,
    And long to see the earth ;
And I am grown world-weary,
    And though I still would bless,
You pout, and shrug your shoulders,
    You frank Adventuress.

And so ride out, my darling,
    This parting is enough ;
The freight you bear is Courage,
    The meed you seek is Love.
Ride far by coast and city,
    An envoy guerdonless,
And seek your fate and find it,
    My own Adventuress.

Good-bye, good-bye, my darling,
    Shake out your gipsy hair ;
The brightness of its blackness,
    Shall fold you from Despair.
Some will be found to love you ;
    And if some hate no less,
Then this shall be your buckler—
    Your laugh, Adventuress.

Your palfrey's nostril widens,
　　His eye rolls proud and bright;
One kiss.—Ten years of living
　　He bears away to-night.
He backs and rears and prances;
　　The spur you lightly press:
A laugh, half-sweet, half-bitter,—
　　Adieu, Adventuress.

Rothesay, 1880.

ENVOI.

I would I had choicer keepsakes,
    For my best is a clumsy thing,
Ill-cut from the opal of pleasure
    And the granite of suffering;

But if amulets you would have of me
    For your guard upon earthly soil,
Take the jewelled burin of laughter,
    And the tempered crowbar of toil.

And, O, think none of my keepsakes—
    Unless you would have me mourn—
But an altar-piece for your saddening,
    Or a whetted barb for your scorn.

For even in the gloomiest corner
    Of my heart's dark graveyard of woes,
I would note but the nestling lilies
    And point but the reaching rose.

And if you should love me a little
    When my story is over and done,
I would pray you, Be kind to children—
    I would pray you, Love the sun.

And when you are sad and weary,
    It may help you—to think of this:
That a sadder soul now leaves you
    With a smile and a wafted kiss.

Amsterdam, 1880.

THE END.

A LIST OF
C. KEGAN PAUL AND CO.'S
PUBLICATIONS.

4.81.

1, *Paternoster Square, London.*

A LIST OF
C. KEGAN PAUL AND CO.'S PUBLICATIONS.

ADAMS (F. O.), F.R.G.S.
The History of Japan. From the Earliest Period to the Present Time. New Edition, revised. 2 volumes. With Maps and Plans. Demy 8vo. Cloth, price 21s. each.

ADAMS (W. D.).
Lyrics of Love, from Shakespeare to Tennyson. Selected and arranged by. Fcap. 8vo. Cloth extra, gilt edges, price 3s. 6d.
Also, a Cheap Edition. Fcap. 8vo. Cloth, price 2s. 6d.

ADAMSON H. T.), B.D.
The Truth as it is in Jesus.
Crown 8vo. Cloth, price 8s. 6d.
The Three Sevens. Crown 8vo. Cloth, price 5s. 6d.

A. K. H. B.
From a Quiet Place. A New Volume of Sermons. Crown 8vo. Cloth, price 5s.

ALBERT (Mary).
Holland and her Heroes to the year 1585. An Adaptation from Motley's "Rise of the Dutch Republic." Small crown 8vo. Cloth, price, 4s. 6d.

ALLEN (Rev. R.), M.A.
Abraham; his Life, Times, and Travels, 3,800 years ago. Second Edition. With Map. Post 8vo. Cloth, price 6s.

ALLEN (Grant), B.A.
Physiological Æsthetics.
Large post 8vo. 9s.

ALLIES (T. W.), M.A.
Per Crucem ad Lucem. The Result of a Life. 2 vols. Demy 8vo. Cloth, price 25s.
A Life's Decision. Crown 8vo. Cloth, price 7s. 6d.

AMATEUR.
A Few Lyrics. Small crown 8vo. Cloth, price 2s.

ANDERSON (Col. R. P.).
Victories and Defeats. An Attempt to explain the Causes which have led to them. An Officer's Manual. Demy 8vo. Cloth, price 14s.

ANDERSON (R. C.), C.E.
Tables for Facilitating the Calculation of every Detail in connection with Earthen and Masonry Dams. Royal 8vo. Cloth, price £2 2s.

Antiope. A Tragedy. Large crown 8vo. Cloth, price 6s.

ARCHER (Thomas).
About my Father's Business. Work amidst the Sick, the Sad, and the Sorrowing. Crown 8vo. Cloth, price 2s. 6d.

Army of the North German Confederation.
A Brief Description of its Organization, of the Different Branches of the Service and their *rôle* in War, of its Mode of Fighting, &c. &c. Translated from the Corrected Edition, by permission of the Author, by Colonel Edward Newdigate. Demy 8vo. Cloth, price 5s.

ARNOLD (Arthur).
Social Politics. Demy 8vo. Cloth, price 14s.
Free Land. Crown 8vo. Cloth, price 6s.

AUBERTIN (J. J.).
Camoens' Lusiads. Portuguese Text, with Translation by. With Map and Portraits. 2 vols. Demy 8vo. Price 30s.

A List of C. Kegan Paul & Co.'s Publications. 3

AUBERTIN (J. J.).—*continued.*
Seventy Sonnets of Camoens'. Portuguese text and translation, with some original poems. Dedicated to Captain Richard F. Burton. Printed on hand-made paper. Cloth, bevelled boards, gilt tops, price 7s. 6d.

Aunt Mary's Bran Pie.
By the author of "St. Olave's." Illustrated. Cloth, price 3s. 6d.

AVIA.
The Odyssey of Homer Done into English Verse. Fcap. 4to. Cloth, price 15s.

BADGER (George Perry), D.C.L.
An English-Arabic Lexicon. In which the equivalents for English words and idiomatic sentences are rendered into literary and colloquial Arabic. Royal 4to. Cloth, price £9 9s.

BAGEHOT (Walter).
Some Articles on the Depreciation of Silver, and Topics connected with it. Demy 8vo. Price 5s.

The English Constitution. A New Edition, Revised and Corrected, with an Introductory Dissertation on Recent Changes and Events. Crown 8vo. Cloth, price 7s. 6d.

Lombard Street. A Description of the Money Market. Seventh Edition. Crown 8vo. Cloth, price 7s. 6d.

BAGOT (Alan).
Accidents in Mines: their Causes and Prevention. Crown 8vo. Cloth, price 6s.

BAKER (Sir Sherston, Bart.).
Halleck's International Law; or Rules Regulating the Intercourse of States in Peace and War. A New Edition, Revised, with Notes and Cases. 2 vols. Demy 8vo. Cloth, price 38s.

The Laws relating to Quarantine. Crown 8vo. Cloth, price 12s. 6d.

BALDWIN (Capt. J. H.), F.Z.S.
The Large and Small Game of Bengal and the North-Western Provinces of India. 4to. With numerous Illustrations. Second Edition. Cloth, price 21s.

BANKS (Mrs. G. L.).
God's Providence House. New Edition. Crown 8vo. Cloth, price 3s. 6d.
Ripples and Breakers. Poems. Square 8vo. Cloth, price 5s.

BARLEE (Ellen).
Locked Out: a Tale of the Strike. With a Frontispiece. Royal 16mo. Cloth, price 1s. 6d.

BARNES (William).
An Outline of English Speechcraft. Crown 8vo. Cloth, price 4s.

Poems of Rural Life, in the Dorset Dialect. New Edition, complete in 1 vol. Crown 8vo. Cloth, price 8s. 6d.

Outlines of Redecraft (Logic). With English Wording. Crown 8vo. Cloth, price 3s.

BARTLEY (George C. T.).
Domestic Economy: Thrift in Every Day Life. Taught in Dialogues suitable for Children of all ages. Small crown 8vo. Cloth, limp, 2s.

BAUR (Ferdinand), Dr. Ph.
A Philological Introduction to Greek and Latin for Students. Translated and adapted from the German of. By C. KEGAN PAUL, M.A. Oxon., and the Rev. E. D. STONE, M.A., late Fellow of King's College, Cambridge, and Assistant Master at Eton. Second and revised edition. Crown 8vo. Cloth, price 6s.

BAYNES (Rev. Canon R. H.).
At the Communion Time. A Manual for Holy Communion. With a preface by the Right Rev. the Lord Bishop of Derry and Raphoe. Cloth, price 1s. 6d.
** Can also be had bound in French morocco, price 2s. 6d.; Persian morocco, price 3s.; Calf, or Turkey morocco, price 3s. 6d.

BAYNES (Rev. Canon R. H.).—*continued.*
Home Songs for Quiet Hours. Fourth and cheaper Edition. Fcap. 8vo. Cloth, price 2s. 6d. *This may also be had handsomely bound in morocco with gilt edges.*

BELLINGHAM (Henry), Barrister-at-Law.
Social Aspects of Catholicism and Protestantism in their Civil Bearing upon Nations. Translated and adapted from the French of M. le Baron de Haulleville. With a Preface by His Eminence Cardinal Manning. Second and cheaper edition. Crown 8vo. Cloth, price 3s. 6d.

BENNETT (Dr. W. C.).
Narrative Poems & Ballads. Fcap. 8vo. Sewed in Coloured Wrapper, price 1s.
Songs for Sailors. Dedicated by Special Request to H. R. H. the Duke of Edinburgh. With Steel Portrait and Illustrations. Crown 8vo. Cloth, price 3s. 6d.
An Edition in Illustrated Paper Covers, price 1s.
Songs of a Song Writer. Crown 8vo. Cloth, price 6s.

BENT (J. Theodore).
Genoa. How the Republic Rose and Fell. With 18 Illustrations. Demy 8vo. Cloth, price 18s.

BETHAM - EDWARDS (Miss M.).
Kitty. With a Frontispiece. Crown 8vo. Cloth, price 6s.

BEVINGTON (L. S.).
Key Notes. Small crown 8vo. Cloth, price 5s.
Blue Roses; or, Helen Malinofska's Marriage. By the Author of "Véra." 2 vols. Fifth Edition. Cloth, gilt tops, 12s.
*** Also a Cheaper Edition in 1 vol. With Frontispiece. Crown 8vo. Cloth, price 6s.

BLUME (Major W.).
The Operations of the German Armies in France, from Sedan to the end of the war of 1870-71. With Map. From the Journals of the Head-quarters Staff. Translated by the late E. M. Jones, Maj. 20th Foot, Prof. of Mil. Hist., Sandhurst. Demy 8vo. Cloth, price 9s.

BOGUSLAWSKI (Capt. A. von).
Tactical Deductions from the War of 1870-71. Translated by Colonel Sir Lumley Graham, Bart., late 18th (Royal Irish) Regiment. Third Edition, Revised and Corrected. Demy 8vo. Cloth, price 7s.

BONWICK (J.), F.R.G.S.
Egyptian Belief and Modern Thought. Large post 8vo. Cloth, price 10s. 6d.
Pyramid Facts and Fancies. Crown 8vo. Cloth, price 5s.
The Tasmanian Lily. With Frontispiece. Crown 8vo. Cloth, price 5s.
Mike Howe, the Bushranger of Van Diemen's Land. With Frontispiece. New and cheaper edition. Crown 8vo. Cloth, price 3s. 6d.

BOWEN (H. C.), M.A.
English Grammar for Beginners. Fcap. 8vo. Cloth, price 1s.
Studies in English, for the use of Modern Schools. Small crown 8vo. Cloth, price 1s. 6d.
Simple English Poems. English Literature for Junior Classes. In Four Parts. Parts I. and II., price 6d. each, now ready.

BOWRING (Sir John).
Autobiographical Recollections. With Memoir by Lewin B. Bowring. Demy 8vo. Price 14s.

Brave Men's Footsteps. By the Editor of "Men who have Risen." A Book of Example and Anecdote for Young People. With Four Illustrations by C. Doyle. Sixth Edition. Crown 8vo. Cloth, price 3s. 6d.

BRIALMONT (Col. A.).
Hasty Intrenchments. Translated by Lieut. Charles A. Empson, R. A. With Nine Plates. Demy 8vo. Cloth, price 6s.

BRIDGETT (Rev. J. E.).
History of the Holy Eucharist in Great Britain. 2 vols., demy 8vo. Cloth, price 18s.

BRODRICK (The Hon. G. C.).
Political Studies. Demy 8vo. Cloth, price 14s.

BROOKE (Rev. S. A.), M. A.
The Late Rev. F. W. Robertson, M.A., Life and Letters of. Edited by.
I. Uniform with the Sermons. 2 vols. With Steel Portrait. Price 7s. 6d.
II. Library Edition. 8vo. With Portrait. Price 12s.
III. A Popular Edition, in 1 vol. 8vo. Price 6s.

Theology in the English Poets. — COWPER, COLERIDGE, WORDSWORTH, and BURNS. Fourth and Cheaper Edition. Post 8vo. Cloth, price 5s.

Christ, in Modern Life. Fourteenth and Cheaper Edition. Crown 8vo. Cloth, price 5s.

Sermons. First Series. Eleventh Edition. Crown 8vo. Cloth, price 6s.

Sermons. Second Series. Third Edition. Crown 8vo. Cloth, price 7s.

The Fight of Faith. Sermons preached on various occasions. Third Edition. Crown 8vo. Cloth, price 7s. 6d.

Frederick Denison Maurice: The Life and Work of. A Memorial Sermon. Crown 8vo. Sewed, price 1s.

BROOKE (W. G.), M.A.
The Public Worship Regulation Act. With a Classified Statement of its Provisions, Notes, and Index. Third Edition, Revised and Corrected. Crown 8vo. Cloth, price 3s. 6d.

Six Privy Council Judgments—1850-1872. Annotated by. Third Edition. Crown 8vo. Cloth, price 9s.

BROUN (J. A.).
Magnetic Observations at Trevandrum and Augustia Malley. Vol. I. 4to. Cloth, price 63s.
The Report from above, separately sewed, price 21s.

BROWN (Rev. J. Baldwin).
The Higher Life. Its Reality, Experience, and Destiny. Fifth and Cheaper Edition. Crown 8vo. Cloth, price 5s.

BROWN (Rev. J. Baldwin)—*continued.*
Doctrine of Annihilation in the Light of the Gospel of Love. Five Discourses. Third Edition. Crown 8vo. Cloth, price 2s. 6d.

The Christian Policy of Life. A Book for Young Men of Business. New and Cheaper Edition. Crown 8vo. Cloth, price 3s. 6d.

BROWN (J. Croumbie), LL.D.
Reboisement in France; or, Records of the Replanting of the Alps, the Cevennes, and the Pyrenees with Trees, Herbage, and Bush. Demy 8vo. Cloth, price 12s. 6d.

The Hydrology of Southern Africa. Demy 8vo. Cloth, price 10s. 6d.

BROWNE (W. R.).
The Inspiration of the New Testament. With a Preface by the Rev. J. P. NORRIS, D.D. Fcap. 8vo. Cloth, price 2s. 6d.

BRYANT (W. C.)
Poems. Red-line Edition. With 24 Illustrations and Portrait of the Author. Crown 8vo. Cloth extra, price 7s. 6d.
A Cheaper Edition, with Frontispiece. Small crown 8vo. Cloth, price 3s. 6d.

BURCKHARDT (Jacob).
The Civilization of the Period of the Renaissance in Italy. Authorized translation, by S. G. C. Middlemore. 2 vols. Demy 8vo. Cloth, price 24s.

BURTON (Mrs. Richard).
The Inner Life of Syria, Palestine, and the Holy Land. With Maps, Photographs, and Coloured Plates. 2 vols. Second Edition. Demy 8vo. Cloth, price 24s.
*** Also a Cheaper Edition in one volume. Large post 8vo. Cloth, price 10s. 6d.

BURTON (Capt. Richard F.).
The Gold Mines of Midian and the Ruined Midianite Cities. A Fortnight's Tour in North Western Arabia. With numerous Illustrations. Second Edition. Demy 8vo. Cloth, price 18s.

BURTON (Capt. Richard F.)—*continued*.
The Land of Midian Revisited. With numerous illustrations on wood and by Chromolithography. 2 vols. Demy 8vo. Cloth, price 32*s*.

BUSBECQ (Ogier Ghiselin de).
His Life and Letters. By Charles Thornton Forster, M.D. and F. H. Blackburne Daniell, M.D. 2 vols. With Frontispieces. Demy 8vo. Cloth, price 24*s*.

BUTLER (Alfred J.).
Amaranth and Asphodel. Songs from the Greek Anthology.— I. Songs of the Love of Women. II. Songs of the Love of Nature. III. Songs of Death. IV. Songs of Hereafter. Small crown 8vo. Cloth, price 2*s*.

CALDERON.
Calderon's Dramas: The Wonder-Working Magician—Life is a Dream—The Purgatory of St. Patrick. Translated by Denis Florence MacCarthy. Post 8vo. Cloth, price 10*s*.

CANDLER (H.).
The Groundwork of Belief. Crown 8vo. Cloth, price 7*s*.

CARPENTER (W. B.), M.D.
The Principles of Mental Physiology. With their Applications to the Training and Discipline of the Mind, and the Study of its Morbid Conditions. Illustrated. Fifth Edition. 8vo. Cloth, price 12*s*.

CARPENTER (Dr. Philip P.).
His Life and Work. Edited by his brother, Russell Lant Carpenter. With portrait and vignette. Second Edition. Crown 8vo. Cloth, price 7*s*. 6*d*.

CAVALRY OFFICER.
Notes on Cavalry Tactics, Organization, &c. With Diagrams Demy 8vo. Cloth, price 12*s*.

CERVANTES.
The Ingenious Knight Don Quixote de la Mancha. A New Translation from the Originals of 1605 and 1608. By A. J. Duffield. With Notes.

CHAPMAN (Hon. Mrs. E. W.).
A Constant Heart. A Story. 2 vols. Cloth, gilt tops, price 12*s*.

CHEYNE (Rev. T. K.).
The Prophecies of Isaiah. Translated, with Critical Notes and Dissertations by. Two vols., demy 8vo. Cloth, price 25*s*.

Children's Toys, and some Elementary Lessons in General Knowledge which they teach. Illustrated. Crown 8vo. Cloth, price 5*s*.

CLAYDEN (P. W.).
England under Lord Beaconsfield. The Political History of the Last Six Years, from the end of 1873 to the beginning of 1880. Second Edition. With Index, and Continuation to March, 1880. Demy 8vo. Cloth, price 16*s*.

CLERY (C.), Lieut.-Col.
Minor Tactics. With 26 Maps and Plans. Fifth and Revised Edition. Demy 8vo. Cloth, price 16*s*.

CLODD (Edward), F.R.A.S.
The Childhood of the World: a Simple Account of Man in Early Times. Sixth Edition. Crown 8vo. Cloth, price 3*s*.
A Special Edition for Schools. Price 1*s*.

The Childhood of Religions. Including a Simple Account of the Birth and Growth of Myths and Legends. Third Thousand. Crown 8vo. Cloth, price 5*s*.
A Special Edition for Schools. Price 1*s*. 6*d*.

Jesus of Nazareth. With a brief Sketch of Jewish History to the Time of His Birth. Small crown 8vo. Cloth, price 6*s*.

COGHLAN (J. Cole), D.D.
The Modern Pharisee and other Sermons. Edited by the Very Rev. A. H. Dickinson, D.D., Dean of Chapel Royal, Dublin. New and cheaper edition. Crown 8vo. Cloth, price 7*s*. 6*d*.

COLERIDGE (Sara).
Pretty Lessons in Verse for Good Children, with some Lessons in Latin, in Easy Rhyme. A New Edition. Illustrated. Fcap. 8vo. Cloth, price 3*s*. 6*d*.

C. Kegan Paul & Co.'s Publications. 7

COLERIDGE (Sara)—*continued*.
Phantasmion. A Fairy Tale.
With an Introductory Preface by the Right Hon. Lord Coleridge, of Ottery St. Mary. A New Edition. Illustrated. Crown 8vo. Cloth, price 7s. 6d.
Memoir and Letters of Sara Coleridge. Edited by her Daughter. Cheap Edition. With one Portrait. Cloth, price 7s. 6d.

COLLINS (Mortimer).
The Secret of Long Life. Small crown 8vo. Cloth, price 3s. 6d.
Inn of Strange Meetings, and other Poems. Crown 8vo. Cloth, price 5s.

COLOMB (Colonel).
The Cardinal Archbishop. A Spanish Legend in twenty-nine Cancions. Small crown 8vo. Cloth, price 5s.

CONNELL (A. K.).
Discontent and Danger in India. Small crown 8vo. Cloth, price 3s. 6d.

CONWAY (Hugh).
A Life's Idylls. Small crown 8vo. Cloth, price 3s. 6d.

COOKE (Prof. J. P.)
Scientific Culture. Crown 8vo. Cloth, price 1s.

COOPER (H. J.).
The Art of Furnishing on Rational and Æsthetic Principles. New and Cheaper Edition. Fcap. 8vo. Cloth, price 1s. 6d.

COPPÉE (François).
L'Exilée. Done into English Verse with the sanction of the Author by I. O. L. Crown 8vo. Vellum, price 5s.

CORFIELD (Prof.), M.D.
Health. Crown 8vo. Cloth, price 6s.

CORY (William).
A Guide to Modern English History. Part I. MDCCCXV.—MDCCCXXX. Demy 8vo. Cloth, price 9s.

COURTNEY (W. L.).
The Metaphysics of John Stuart Mill. Crown 8vo. Cloth, price 5s. 6d.

COWAN (Rev. William).
Poems : Chiefly Sacred, including Translations from some Ancient Latin Hymns. Fcap. 8vo. Cloth, price 5s.

COX (Rev. Sir G. W.), Bart.
A History of Greece from the Earliest Period to the end of the Persian War. New Edition. 2 vols. Demy 8vo. Cloth, price 36s.
The Mythology of the Aryan Nations. New Edition. 2 vols. Demy 8vo. Cloth, price 28s.
A General History of Greece from the Earliest Period to the Death of Alexander the Great, with a sketch of the subsequent History to the present time. New Edition. Crown 8vo. Cloth, price 7s. 6d.
Tales of Ancient Greece. New Edition. Small crown 8vo Cloth, price 6s.
School History of Greece. With Maps. New Edition. Fcap 8vo. Cloth, price 3s. 6d.
The Great Persian War from the Histories of Herodotus. New Edition. Fcap. 8vo. Cloth, price 3s. 6d.
A Manual of Mythology in the form of Question and Answer New Edition. Fcap. 8vo. Cloth, price 3s.

COX (Rev. Sir G. W.), Bart., M.A., and **EUSTACE HINTON JONES.**
Popular Romances of the Middle Ages. Second Edition in one volume. Crown 8vo. Cloth, price 6s.

COX (Rev. Samuel).
A Commentary on the Book of Job. With a Translation. Demy 8vo. Cloth, price 15s.
Salvator Mundi ; or, Is Christ the Saviour of all Men? Sixth Edition. Crown 8vo. Cloth, price 5s.
The Genesis of Evil, and other Sermons, mainly Expository. Second Edition. Crown 8vo. Cloth, price 6s.

CRAUFURD (A. H.).
Seeking for Light : Sermons. Crown 8vo. Cloth, price 5s.

CRAVEN (Mrs.).
A Year's Meditations.
Crown 8vo. Cloth, price 6s.

CRAWFURD (Oswald).
Portugal, Old and New.
With Illustrations and Maps. Demy 8vo. Cloth, price 16s.

CRESSWELL (Mrs. G.).
The King's Banner. Drama in Four Acts. Five Illustrations. 4to. Cloth, price 10s. 6d.

CROMPTON (Henry).
Industrial Conciliation.
Fcap. 8vo. Cloth, price 2s. 6d.

CROZIER (John Beattie), M.B.
The Religion of the Future.
Crown 8vo. Cloth, price 6s.

DALTON (John Neale), M.A., R.N.
Sermons to Naval Cadets.
Preached on board H.M.S. "Britannia." Second Edition. Small crown 8vo. Cloth, price 3s. 6d.

D'ANVERS (N. R.).
Parted. A Tale of Clouds and Sunshine. With 4 Illustrations. Extra Fcap. 8vo. Cloth, price 3s. 6d.

Little Minnie's Troubles.
An Every-day Chronicle. With Four Illustrations by W. H. Hughes. Fcap. Cloth, price 3s. 6d.

Pixie's Adventures; or, the Tale of a Terrier. With 21 Illustrations. 16mo. Cloth, price 4s. 6d.

Nanny's Adventures; or, the Tale of a Goat. With 12 Illustrations. 16mo. Cloth, price 4s. 6d.

DAVIDSON (Rev. Samuel), D.D., LL.D.
The New Testament, translated from the Latest Greek Text of Tischendorf. A New and thoroughly Revised Edition. Post 8vo. Cloth, price 10s. 6d.

Canon of the Bible: Its Formation, History, and Fluctuations. Third Edition, revised and enlarged. Small crown 8vo. Cloth, price 5s.

DAVIES (G. Christopher).
Rambles and Adventures of Our School Field Club. With Four Illustrations. Crown 8vo. Cloth, price 5s.

DAVIES (Rev. J. L.), M.A.
Theology and Morality.
Essays on Questions of Belief and Practice. Crown 8vo. Cloth, price 7s. 6d.

DAVIES (T. Hart.).
Catullus. Translated into English Verse. Crown 8vo. Cloth, price 6s.

DAWSON (George), M.A.
Prayers, with a Discourse on Prayer. Edited by his Wife. Fifth Edition. Crown 8vo. Price 6s.

Sermons on Disputed Points and Special Occasions. Edited by his Wife. Third Edition. Crown 8vo. Cloth, price 6s.

Sermons on Daily Life and Duty. Edited by his Wife. Second Edition. Crown 8vo. Cloth, price 6s.

DE L'HOSTE (Col. E. P.).
The Desert Pastor, Jean Jarousseau. Translated from the French of Eugène Pelletan. With a Frontispiece. New Edition. Fcap. 8vo. Cloth, price 3s. 6d.

DENNIS (J.).
English Sonnets. Collected and Arranged. Fcap. 8vo. Cloth, price 2s. 6d.

DE REDCLIFFE (Viscount Stratford), P.C., K.G., G.C.B.
Why am I a Christian?
Fifth Edition. Crown 8vo. Cloth, price 3s.

DESPREZ (Philip S.).
Daniel and John; or, the Apocalypse of the Old and that of the New Testament. Demy 8vo. Cloth, price 12s.

DE TOCQUEVILLE (A.).
Correspondence and Conversations of, with Nassau William Senior, from 1834 to 1859. Edited by M. C. M. Simpson. 2 vols. Post 8vo. Cloth, price 21s.

DE VERE (Aubrey).
Legends of the Saxon Saints. Small crown 8vo. Cloth, price 6s.

Alexander the Great. A Dramatic Poem. Small crown 8vo. Cloth, price 5s.

The Infant Bridal, and other Poems. A New and Enlarged Edition. Fcap. 8vo. Cloth, price 7s. 6d.

The Legends of St. Patrick, and other Poems. Small crown 8vo. Cloth, price 5s.

St. Thomas of Canterbury. A Dramatic Poem. Large fcap. 8vo. Cloth, price 5s.

Antar and Zara: an Eastern Romance. INISFAIL, and other Poems, Meditative and Lyrical. Fcap. 8vo. Price 6s.

The Fall of Rora, the Search after Proserpine, and other Poems, Meditative and Lyrical. Fcap. 8vo. Price 6s.

DOBELL (Mrs. Horace).
Ethelstone, Eveline, and other Poems. Crown 8vo. Cloth, price 6s.

DOBSON (Austin).
Vignettes in Rhyme and Vers de Société. Third Edition. Fcap. 8vo. Cloth, price 5s.

Proverbs in Porcelain. By the Author of "Vignettes in Rhyme." Second Edition. Crown 8vo. 6s.

Dolores. A Theme with Variations. In three parts. Small crown 8vo. Cloth, price 5s.

Dorothy. A Country Story in Elegiac Verse. With Preface. Demy 8vo. Cloth, price 5s.

DOWDEN (Edward), LL.D.
Shakspere: a Critical Study of his Mind and Art. Fifth Edition. Large post 8vo. Cloth, price 12s.

Studies in Literature, 1789-1877. Large post 8vo. Cloth, price 12s.

Poems. Second Edition. Fcap. 8vo. Cloth, price 5s.

DOWNTON (Rev. H.), M.A.
Hymns and Verses. Original and Translated. Small crown 8vo. Cloth, price 3s. 6d.

DREWRY (G. O.), M.D.
The Common-Sense Management of the Stomach. Fifth Edition. Fcap. 8vo. Cloth, price 2s. 6d.

DREWRY (G. O.), M.D., and BARTLETT (H. C.), Ph.D., F.C.S.
Cup and Platter: or, Notes on Food and its Effects. New and cheaper Edition. Small 8vo. Cloth, price 1s. 6d.

DRUMMOND (Miss).
Tripps Buildings. A Study from Life, with Frontispiece. Small crown 8vo. Cloth, price 3s. 6d.

DU MONCEL (Count).
The Telephone, the Microphone, and the Phonograph. With 74 Illustrations. Small crown 8vo. Cloth, price 5s.

DUTT (Toru).
A Sheaf Gleaned in French Fields. New Edition, with Portrait. Demy 8vo. Cloth, price 10s. 6d.

DU VERNOIS (Col. von Verdy).
Studies in leading Troops. An authorized and accurate Translation by Lieutenant H. J. T. Hildyard, 71st Foot. Parts I. and II. Demy 8vo. Cloth, price 7s.

EDEN (Frederick).
The Nile without a Dragoman. Second Edition. Crown 8vo. Cloth, price 7s. 6d.

EDIS (Robert W.).
Decoration and Furniture of Town Houses. A series of Cantor Lectures delivered before the Society of Arts, 1880. Second Edition, amplified and enlarged, with 29 full-page Illustrations and numerous sketches. Square 8vo. Cloth, price 12s. 6d.

EDMONDS (Herbert).
Well Spent Lives: a Series of Modern Biographies. Crown 8vo. Price 5s.

A 2

Educational Code of the Prussian Nation, in its Present Form. In accordance with the Decisions of the Common Provincial Law, and with those of Recent Legislation. Crown 8vo. Cloth, price 2s. 6d.

EDWARDS (Rev. Basil).

Minor Chords; or, Songs for the Suffering: a Volume of Verse. Fcap. 8vo. Cloth, price 3s. 6d.; paper, price 2s. 6d.

ELLIOT (Lady Charlotte).

Medusa and other Poems. Crown 8vo. Cloth, price 6s.

ELLIOTT (Ebenezer), The Corn-Law Rhymer.

Poems. Edited by his Son, the Rev. Edwin Elliott, of St. John's, Antigua. 2 vols. Crown 8vo. Cloth, price 18s.

ELSDALE (Henry).

Studies in Tennyson's Idylls. Crown 8vo. Cloth, price 5s.

ELYOT (Sir Thomas).

The Boke named the Gouernour. Edited from the First Edition of 1531 by Henry Herbert Stephen Croft, M.A., Barrister-at-Law. With Portraits of Sir Thomas and Lady Elyot, copied by permission of her Majesty from Holbein's Original Drawings at Windsor Castle. 2 vols. fcap. 4to. Cloth, price 50s.

English Odes, selected by Edmund W. Gosse. With Frontispiece by Hamo Thornycroft. Parchment, 6s.; vellum, 7s. 6d.

Epic of Hades (The). By the author of "Songs of Two Worlds." Twelfth Edition. Fcap. 8vo. Cloth, price 7s. 6d.
*** Also an Illustrated Edition with seventeen full-page designs in photomezzotint by GEORGE R. CHAPMAN. 4to. Cloth, extra gilt leaves, price 25s, and a Large Paper Edition, with portrait, price 10s. 6d.

EVANS (Anne).

Poems and Music. With Memorial Preface by Ann Thackeray Ritchie. Large crown 8vo. Cloth, price 7s. 6d.

EVANS (Mark).

The Gospel of Home Life. Crown 8vo. Cloth, price 4s. 6d.

The Story of our Father's Love, told to Children. Fourth and Cheaper Edition. With Four Illustrations. Fcap. 8vo. Cloth, price 1s. 6d.

A Book of Common Prayer and Worship for Household Use, compiled exclusively from the Holy Scriptures. New and Cheaper Edition. Fcap. 8vo. Cloth, price 1s.

The King's Story Book. In three parts. Fcap. 8vo. Cloth, price 1s. 6d. each.
*** Parts I. and II., with eight illustrations and two Picture Maps, now ready.

EX-CIVILIAN.

Life in the Mofussil; or, Civilian Life in Lower Bengal. 2 vols. Large post 8vo. Price 14s.

FARQUHARSON (M.).

I. **Elsie Dinsmore.** Crown 8vo. Cloth, price 3s. 6d.

II. **Elsie's Girlhood.** Crown 8vo. Cloth, price 3s. 6d.

III. **Elsie's Holidays at Roselands.** Crown 8vo. Cloth, price 3s. 6d.

FIELD (Horace), B.A. Lond.

The Ultimate Triumph of Christianity. Small crown 8vo. Cloth, price 3s. 6d.

FINN (the late James), M.R.A.S.

Stirring Times; or, Records from Jerusalem Consular Chronicles of 1853 to 1856. Edited and Compiled by his Widow. With a Preface by the Viscountess STRANGFORD. 2 vols. Demy 8vo. Price 30s.

Folkestone Ritual Case (The). The Argument, Proceedings Judgment, and Report, revised by the several Counsel engaged. Demy 8vo. Cloth, price 25s.

FORMBY (Rev. Henry).
Ancient Rome and its Connection with the Christian Religion: an Outline of the History of the City from its First Foundation down to the Erection of the Chair of St. Peter, A.D. 42-47. With numerous Illustrations of Ancient Monuments, Sculpture, and Coinage, and of the Antiquities of the Christian Catacombs. Royal 4to. Cloth extra, price 50s. Roxburgh, half-morocco, price 52s. 6d.

FOWLE (Rev. T. W.), M.A.
The Reconciliation of Religion and Science. Being Essays on Immortality, Inspiration, Miracles, and the Being of Christ. Demy 8vo. Cloth, price 10s. 6d.

The Divine Legation of Christ. Crown 8vo. Cloth, price 7s.

FRASER (Donald).
Exchange Tables of Sterling and Indian Rupee Currency, upon a new and extended system, embracing Values from One Farthing to One Hundred Thousand Pounds, and at Rates progressing, in Sixteenths of a Penny, from 1s. 9d. to 2s. 3d. per Rupee. Royal 8vo. Cloth, price 10s. 6d.

FRISWELL (J. Hain).
The Better Self. Essays for Home Life. Crown 8vo. Cloth, price 6s.

One of Two; or, A Left-Handed Bride. With a Frontispiece. Crown 8vo. Cloth, price 3s. 6d.

GARDNER (J.), M.D.
Longevity: The Means of Prolonging Life after Middle Age. Fourth Edition, Revised and Enlarged. Small crown 8vo. Cloth, price 4s.

GARRETT (E.).
By Still Waters. A Story for Quiet Hours. With Seven Illustrations. Crown 8vo. Cloth, price 6s.

GEBLER (Karl Von).
Galileo Galilei and the Roman Curia, from Authentic Sources. Translated with the sanction of the Author, by Mrs. GEORGE STURGE. Demy 8vo. Cloth, price 12s.

GEDDES (James).
History of the Administration of John de Witt, Grand Pensionary of Holland. Vol. I. 1623—1654. Demy 8vo., with Portrait. Cloth, price 15s.

GEORGE (Henry).
Progress and Poverty. An Inquiry into the Cause of Industrial Depressions and of Increase of Want with Increase of Wealth. The Remedy. Post 8vo. Cloth, price 7s. 6d.

G. H. T.
Verses, mostly written in India. Crown 8vo. Cloth, price 6s.

GILBERT (Mrs.).
Autobiography and other Memorials. Edited by Josiah Gilbert. Third Edition. With Portrait and several Wood Engravings. Crown 8vo. Cloth, price 7s. 6d.

GILL (Rev. W. W.), B.A.
Myths and Songs from the South Pacific. With a Preface by F. Max Müller, M.A., Professor of Comparative Philology at Oxford. Post 8vo. Cloth, price 9s.

Ginevra and The Duke of Guise. Two Tragedies. Crown 8vo. Cloth, price 6s.

GLOVER (F.), M.A.
Exempla Latina. A First Construing Book with Short Notes, Lexicon, and an Introduction to the Analysis of Sentences. Fcap. 8vo. Cloth, price 2s.

GODWIN (William).
William Godwin: His Friends and Contemporaries. With Portraits and Facsimiles of the handwriting of Godwin and his Wife. By C. Kegan Paul. 2 vols. Demy 8vo. Cloth, price 28s.

The Genius of Christianity Unveiled. Being Essays never before published. Edited, with a Preface, by C. Kegan Paul. Crown 8vo. Cloth, price 7s. 6d.

GOETZE (Capt. A. von).
Operations of the German Engineers during the War of 1870-1871. Published by Authority, and in accordance with Official Documents. Translated from the German by Colonel G. Graham, V.C., C.B., R.E. With 6 large Maps. Demy 8vo. Cloth, price 21s.

GOLDSMID (Sir Francis Henry).
Memoir of. With Portrait.
Crown 8vo. Cloth, price 5s.

GOODENOUGH (Commodore J. G.), R.N., C.B., C.M.G.
Memoir of, with Extracts from his Letters and Journals. Edited by his Widow. With Steel Engraved Portrait. Square 8vo. Cloth, 5s.
* Also a Library Edition with Maps, Woodcuts, and Steel Engraved Portrait. Square post 8vo. Cloth, price 14s.

GOSSE (Edmund W.).
Studies in the Literature of Northern Europe. With a Frontispiece designed and etched by Alma Tadema. Large post 8vo. Cloth, price 12s.

New Poems. Crown 8vo. Cloth, price 7s. 6d.

GOULD (Rev. S. Baring), M.A.
Germany, Present and Past.
2 Vols. Demy 8vo. Cloth, price 21s.

The Vicar of Morwenstow: a Memoir of the Rev. R. S. Hawker. With Portrait. Third Edition, revised. Square post 8vo. Cloth, 10s. 6d.

GREENOUGH (Mrs. Richard).
Mary Magdalene : A Poem. Large post 8vo. Parchment antique, price 6s.

GRIFFITH (Thomas), A.M.
The Gospel of the Divine Life. A Study of the Fourth Evangelist. Demy 8vo. Cloth, price 14s.

GRIMLEY (Rev. H. N.), M.A.
Tremadoc Sermons, chiefly on the SPIRITUAL BODY, the UNSEEN WORLD, and the DIVINE HUMANITY. Second Edition. Crown 8vo. Cloth, price 6s.

GRÜNER (M. L.).
Studies of Blast Furnace Phenomena. Translated by L. D. B. Gordon, F.R.S.E., F.G.S. Demy 8vo. Cloth, price 7s. 6d.

GURNEY (Rev. Archer).
Words of Faith and Cheer. A Mission of Instruction and Suggestion. Crown 8vo. Cloth, price 6s.

Gwen : A Drama in Monologue. By the Author of the "Epic of Hades." Second Edition. Fcap. 8vo. Cloth, price 5s.

HAECKEL (Prof. Ernst).
The History of Creation. Translation revised by Professor E. Ray Lankester, M.A., F.R.S. With Coloured Plates and Genealogical Trees of the various groups of both plants and animals. 2 vols. Second Edition. Post 8vo. Cloth, price 32s.

The History of the Evolution of Man. With numerous Illustrations. 2 vols. Large post 8vo. Cloth, price 32s.

Freedom in Science and Teaching. From the German of Ernst Haeckel, with a Prefatory Note by T. H. Huxley, F.R.S. Crown 8vo. Cloth, price 5s.

HAKE (A. Egmont).
Paris Originals, with twenty etchings, by Léon Richeton. Large post 8vo. Cloth, price 14s.

Halleck's International Law ; or, Rules Regulating the Intercourse of States in Peace and War. A New Edition, revised, with Notes and Cases. By Sir Sherston Baker, Bart. 2 vols. Demy 8vo. Cloth, price 38s.

HARDY (Thomas).
A Pair of Blue Eyes. New Edition. With Frontispiece. Crown 8vo. Cloth, price 6s.

The Return of the Native. New Edition. With Frontispiece. Crown 8vo. Cloth, price 6s.

HARRISON (Lieut.-Col. R.).
The Officer's Memorandum Book for Peace and War. Third Edition. Oblong 32mo. roan, with pencil, price 3s. 6d.

HARTINGTON (The Right Hon. the Marquis of), M.P.
Election Speeches in 1879 and 1880. With Address to the Electors of North-East Lancashire. Crown 8vo. Cloth, price 3s. 6d.

HAWEIS (Rev. H. R.), M.A.
Arrows in the Air. Crown 8vo. Second Edition. Cloth, price 6s.

HAWEIS (Rev. H. R.), M.A.— *continued.*
Current Coin. Materialism—The Devil—Crime—Drunkenness—Pauperism—Emotion—Recreation—The Sabbath. Third Edition. Crown 8vo. Cloth, price 6s.
Speech in Season. Fourth Edition. Crown 8vo. Cloth, price 9s.
Thoughts for the Times. Eleventh Edition. Crown 8vo. Cloth, price 7s. 6d.
Unsectarian Family Prayers. New and Cheaper Edition. Fcap. 8vo. Cloth, price 1s. 6d.

HAWKER (Robert Stephen).
The Poetical Works of. Now first collected and arranged with a prefatory notice by J. G. Godwin. With Portrait. Crown 8vo. Cloth, price 12s.

HAWKINS (Edwards Comerford).
Spirit and Form. Sermons preached in the parish church of Leatherhead. Crown 8vo. Cloth, price 6s.

HAWTREY (Edward M.).
Corydalis. A Story of the Sicilian Expedition. Small crown 8vo. Cloth, price 3s. 6d.

HAYES (A. H.).
New Colorado and the Santa Fé Trail. With map and 60 Illustrations. Crown 8vo. Cloth, price 9s.

HEIDENHAIN (Rudolf), M.D.
Animal Magnetism. Physiological Observations. Translated from the Fourth German Edition, by L. C. Wooldridge. With a Preface by G. R. Romanes, F.R.S. Crown 8vo. Cloth, price 2s. 6d.

HELLWALD (Baron F. von).
The Russians in Central Asia. A Critical Examination, down to the present time, of the Geography and History of Central Asia. Translated by Lieut.-Col. Theodore Wirgman, LL.B. Large post 8vo. With Map. Cloth, price 12s.

HELVIG (Major H.).
The Operations of the Bavarian Army Corps. Translated by Captain G. S. Schwabe. With Five large Maps. In 2 vols. Demy 8vo. Cloth, price 24s.

HELVIG (Major H.).—*continued.*
Tactical Examples: Vol. I. The Battalion, price 15s. Vol. II. The Regiment and Brigade, price 10s. 6d. Translated from the German by Col. Sir Lumley Graham. With numerous Diagrams. Demy 8vo. Cloth.

HERFORD (Brooke)..
The Story of Religion in England. A Book for Young Folk. Crown 8vo. Cloth, price 5s.

HINTON (James).
Life and Letters of. Edited by Ellice Hopkins, with an Introduction by Sir W. W. Gull, Bart., and Portrait engraved on Steel by C. H. Jeens. Second Edition. Crown 8vo. Cloth, 8s. 6d.
Chapters on the Art of Thinking, and other Essays. With an Introduction by Shadworth Hodgson. Edited by C. H. Hinton. Crown 8vo. Cloth, price 8s. 6d.
The Place of the Physician. To which is added ESSAYS ON THE LAW OF HUMAN LIFE, AND ON THE RELATION BETWEEN ORGANIC AND INORGANIC WORLDS. Second Edition. Crown 8vo. Cloth, price 3s. 6d.
Physiology for Practical Use. By various Writers. With 50 Illustrations. Third and cheaper edition. Crown 8vo. Cloth, price 5s.
An Atlas of Diseases of the Membrana Tympani. With Descriptive Text. Post 8vo. Price £6 6s.
The Questions of Aural Surgery. With Illustrations. 2 vols. Post 8vo. Cloth, price 12s. 6d.
The Mystery of Pain. New Edition. Fcap. 8vo. Cloth limp, 1s.

HOCKLEY (W. B.).
Tales of the Zenana; or, A Nuwab's Leisure Hours. By the Author of "Pandurang Hari." With a Preface by Lord Stanley of Alderley. 2 vols. Crown 8vo. Cloth, price 21s.
Pandurang Hari; or, Memoirs of a Hindoo. A Tale of Mahratta Life sixty years ago. With a Preface by Sir H. Bartle E. Frere, G.C.S.I., &c. New and Cheaper Edition. Crown 8vo. Cloth, price 6s.

HOFFBAUER (Capt.).
The German Artillery in the Battles near Metz. Based on the official reports of the German Artillery. Translated by Capt. E. O. Hollist. With Map and Plans. Demy 8vo. Cloth, price 21s.

HOLMES (E. G. A.).
Poems. First and Second Series. Fcap. 8vo. Cloth, price 5s. each.

HOOPER (Mary).
Little Dinners: How to Serve them with Elegance and Economy. Thirteenth Edition. Crown 8vo. Cloth, price 5s.
Cookery for Invalids, Persons of Delicate Digestion, and Children. Crown 8vo. Cloth, price 3s. 6d.
Every-Day Meals. Being Economical and Wholesome Recipes for Breakfast, Luncheon, and Supper. Second Edition. Crown 8vo. Cloth, price 5s.

HOOPER (Mrs. G.).
The House of Raby. With a Frontispiece. Crown 8vo. Cloth, price 3s. 6d.

HOPKINS (Ellice).
Life and Letters of James Hinton, with an Introduction by Sir W. W. Gull, Bart., and Portrait engraved on Steel by C. H. Jeens. Second Edition. Crown 8vo. Cloth price 8s. 6d.

HOPKINS (M.).
The Port of Refuge; or, Counsel and Aid to Shipmasters in Difficulty, Doubt, or Distress. Crown 8vo. Second and Revised Edition. Cloth, price 6s.

HORNER (The Misses).
Walks in Florence. A New and thoroughly Revised Edition. 2 vols. Crown 8vo. Cloth limp. With Illustrations.
   Vol. I.—Churches, Streets, and Palaces. 10s. 6d. Vol. II.—Public Galleries and Museums. 5s.

HULL (Edmund C. P.).
The European in India. With a MEDICAL GUIDE FOR ANGLO-INDIANS. By R. R. S. Mair, M.D., F.R.C.S.E. Third Edition, Revised and Corrected. Post 8vo. Cloth, price 6s.

HUTCHISON (Lieut.-Col. F. J.), and Capt. G. H. MACGREGOR.
Military Sketching and Reconnaissance. With Fifteen Plates. Second edition. Small 8vo. Cloth, price 6s.
The first Volume of Military Handbooks for Regimental Officers. Edited by Lient.-Col. C. B. BRACKENBURY, R.A., A.A.G.

HUTTON (Arthur), M.A.
The Anglican Ministry. Its Nature and Value in relation to the Catholic Priesthood. With a Preface by his Eminence Cardinal Newman. Demy 8vo. Cloth, price 14s.

INCHBOLD (J. W.).
Annus Amoris. Sonnets. Fcap. 8vo. Cloth, price 4s. 6d.

INGELOW (Jean).
Off the Skelligs. A Novel. With Frontispiece. Second Edition. Crown 8vo. Cloth, price 6s.
The Little Wonder-horn. A Second Series of "Stories Told to a Child." With Fifteen Illustrations. Small 8vo. Cloth, price 2s. 6d.

Indian Bishoprics. By an Indian Churchman. Demy 8vo. 6d.

International Scientific Series (The).
I. **Forms of Water:** A Familiar Exposition of the Origin and Phenomena of Glaciers. By J. Tyndall, LL.D., F.R.S. With 25 Illustrations. Seventh Edition. Crown 8vo. Cloth, price 5s.
II. **Physics and Politics;** or, Thoughts on the Application of the Principles of "Natural Selection" and "Inheritance" to Political Society. By Walter Bagehot. Fifth Edition. Crown 8vo. Cloth, price 4s.
III. **Foods.** By Edward Smith, M.D., &c. With numerous Illustrations. Seventh Edition. Crown 8vo. Cloth, price 5s.
IV. **Mind and Body:** The Theories of their Relation. By Alexander Bain, LL.D. With Four Illustrations. Tenth Edition. Crown 8vo. Cloth, price 4s.
V. **The Study of Sociology.** By Herbert Spencer. Eighth Edition. Crown 8vo. Cloth, price 5s.

International Scientific Series (The)—*continued*.

VI. **On the Conservation of Energy.** By Balfour Stewart, LL.D., &c. With 14 Illustrations. Fifth Edition. Crown 8vo. Cloth, price 5s.

VII. **Animal Locomotion; or, Walking, Swimming, and Flying.** By J. B. Pettigrew, M.D., &c. With 130 Illustrations. Second Edition. Crown 8vo. Cloth, price 5s.

VIII. **Responsibility in Mental Disease.** By Henry Maudsley, M.D. Third Edition. Crown 8vo. Cloth, price 5s.

IX. **The New Chemistry.** By Professor J. P. Cooke. With 31 Illustrations. Fifth Edition. Crown 8vo. Cloth, price 5s.

X. **The Science of Law.** By Prof. Sheldon Amos. Fourth Edition. Crown 8vo. Cloth, price 5s.

XI. **Animal Mechanism.** A Treatise on Terrestrial and Aerial Locomotion. By Prof. E. J. Marey. With 117 Illustrations. Second Edition. Crown 8vo. Cloth, price 5s.

XII. **The Doctrine of Descent and Darwinism.** By Prof. Osca Schmidt. With 26 Illustrations. Third Edition. Crown 8vo. Cloth, price 5s.

XIII. **The History of the Conflict between Religion and Science.** By J. W. Draper, M.D., LL.D. Fourteenth Edition. Crown 8vo. Cloth, price 5s.

XIV. **Fungi; their Nature, Influences, Uses, &c.** By M. C. Cooke, LL.D. Edited by the Rev. M. J. Berkeley, F.L.S. With numerous Illustrations. Second Edition. Crown 8vo. Cloth, price 5s.

XV. **The Chemical Effects of Light and Photography.** By Dr. Hermann Vogel. With 100 Illustrations. Third and Revised Edition. Crown 8vo. Cloth, price 5s.

XVI. **The Life and Growth of Language.** By Prof. William Dwight Whitney. Second Edition. Crown 8vo. Cloth, price 5s.

XVII. **Money and the Mechanism of Exchange.** By W. Stanley Jevons, F.R.S. Fourth Edition. Crown 8vo. Cloth, price 5s.

International Scientific Series (The)—*continued*.

XVIII. **The Nature of Light:** With a General Account of Physical Optics. By Dr. Eugene Lommel. With 188 Illustrations and a table of Spectra in Chromo-lithography. Third Edition. Crown 8vo. Cloth, price 5s.

XIX. **Animal Parasites and Messmates.** By M. Van Beneden. With 83 Illustrations. Second Edition. Crown 8vo. Cloth, price 5s.

XX. **Fermentation.** By Prof. Schützenberger. With 28 Illustrations. Third Edition. Crown 8vo. Cloth, price 5s.

XXI. **The Five Senses of Man.** By Prof. Bernstein. With 91 Illustrations. Second Edition. Crown 8vo. Cloth, price 5s.

XXII. **The Theory of Sound in its Relation to Music.** By Prof. Pietro Blaserna. With numerous Illustrations. Second Edition. Crown 8vo. Cloth, price 5s.

XXIII. **Studies in Spectrum Analysis.** By J. Norman Lockyer. F.R.S. With six photographic Illustrations of Spectra, and numerous engravings on wood. Crown 8vo. Second Edition. Cloth, price 6s. 6d.

XXIV. **A History of the Growth of the Steam Engine.** By Prof. R. H. Thurston. With numerous Illustrations. Second Edition. Crown 8vo. Cloth, price 6s. 6d.

XXV. **Education as a Science.** By Alexander Bain, LL.D. Third Edition. Crown 8vo. Cloth, price 5s.

XXVI. **The Human Species.** By Prof. A. de Quatrefages. Third Edition. Crown 8vo. Cloth, price 5s.

XXVII. **Modern Chromatics.** With Applications to Art and Industry, by Ogden N. Rood. Second Edition. With 130 original Illustrations. Crown 8vo. Cloth, price 5s.

XXVIII. **The Crayfish:** an Introduction to the Study of Zoology. By Prof. T. H. Huxley. Second edition. With eighty-two Illustrations. Crown 8vo. Cloth, price 5s.

XXIX. **The Brain as an Organ of Mind.** By H. Charlton Bastian, M.D. With numerous Illustrations. Second Edition. Crown 8vo. Cloth, price 5s.

International Scientific Series (The)—*continued*.
XXX. The Atomic Theory. By Prof. Ad. Wurtz. Translated by E. Clemin-Shaw. Second Edition. Crown 8vo. Cloth, price 5s.
XXXI. The Natural Conditions of Existence as they affect Animal Life. By Karl Semper. Second Edition. Crown 8vo. Cloth, price 5s.
XXXII. General Physiology of Muscles and Nerves. By Prof. J. Rosenthal. Second Edition, with illustrations. Crown 8vo. Cloth, price 5s.
XXXIII. Sight: an Exposition of the Principles of Monocular and Binocular Vision. By Joseph Le Conte, LL.D. With numerous illustrations. Crown 8vo. Cloth, price 5s.

JENKIN (Rev. Canon).
The Girdle Legend of Prato. Small crown 8vo. Cloth, price 2s.

JENKINS (E.) and RAYMOND (J.).
The Architect's Legal Handbook. Third Edition Revised. Crown 8vo. Cloth, price 6s.

JENKINS (Rev. R. C.), M.A.
The Privilege of Peter and the Claims of the Roman Church confronted with the Scriptures, the Councils, and the Testimony of the Popes themselves. Fcap. 8vo. Cloth, price 3s. 6d.

JENNINGS (Mrs. Vaughan).
Rahel: Her Life and Letters. With a Portrait from the Painting by Daffinger. Square post 8vo. Cloth, price 7s. 6d.

Jeroveam's Wife and other Poems. Fcap. 8vo. Cloth, price 3s. 6d.

JOEL (L.).
A Consul's Manual and Shipowner's and Shipmaster's Practical Guide in their Transactions Abroad. With Definitions of Nautical, Mercantile, and Legal Terms; a Glossary of Mercantile Terms in English, French, German, Italian, and Spanish. Tables of the Money, Weights, and Measures of the Principal Commercial Nations and their Equivalents in British Standards; and Forms of Consular and Notarial Acts. Demy 8vo. Cloth, price 12s.

JOHNSON (Virginia W.).
The Catskill Mountains. Illustrated by Alfred Fredericks. Cloth, price 5s.

JOHNSTONE (C. F.), M.A.
Historical Abstracts. Being Outlines of the History of some of the less-known States of Europe. Crown 8vo. Cloth, price 7s. 6d.

JONES (Lucy).
Puddings and Sweets. Being Three Hundred and Sixty-Five Receipts approved by Experience. Crown 8vo., price 2s. 6d.

JOYCE (P. W.), LL.D., &c.
Old Celtic Romances. Translated from the Gaelic by. Crown 8vo. Cloth, price 7s. 6d.

KAUFMANN (Rev. M.), B.A.
Utopias; or, Schemes of Social Improvement, from Sir Thomas More to Karl Marx. Crown 8vo. Cloth, price 5s.

Socialism: Its Nature, its Dangers, and its Remedies considered. Crown 8vo. Cloth, price 7s. 6d.

KAY (Joseph), M.A., Q.C.
Free Trade in Land. Edited by his Widow. With Preface by the Right Hon. John Bright, M.P. Sixth Edition. Crown 8vo. Cloth, price 5s.

KEMPIS (Thomas À).
OF THE IMITATION OF CHRIST. A revised Translation, choicely printed on handmade paper, with a Miniature Frontispiece on India paper from a design by W. B. Richmond. Limp parchment, antique, price 6s.; vellum, price 7s. 6d.

KENT (Carolo).
Carona Catholica ad Petri successoris Pedes Oblata. De Summi Pontificis Leonis XIII. Assumptione Epiggramma. In Quinquaginta Linguis. Fcap. 4to. Cloth, price 15s.

KER (David).
The Boy Slave in Bokhara. A Tale of Central Asia. With Illustrations. Crown 8vo. Cloth, price 3s. 6d.

The Wild Horseman of the Pampas. Illustrated. Crown 8vo. Cloth, price 3s. 6d.

KERNER (Dr. A.), Professor of Botany in the University of Innsbruck.
Flowers and their Unbidden Guests. Translation edited by W. OGLE, M.A., M.D., and a prefatory letter by C. Darwin, F.R.S. With Illustrations. Sq. 8vo. Cloth, price 9s.

KIDD (Joseph), M.D.
The Laws of Therapeutics, or, the Science and Art of Medicine. Second Edition. Crown 8vo. Cloth, price 6s.

KINAHAN (G. Henry), M.R.I.A., &c., of her Majesty's Geological Survey.
Manual of the Geology of Ireland. With 8 Plates, 26 Woodcuts, and a Map of Ireland, geologically coloured. Square 8vo. Cloth, price 15s.

KING (Mrs. Hamilton).
The Disciples. Fourth Edition, with Portrait and Notes. Crown 8vo. Cloth, price 7s. 6d.
Aspromonte, and other Poems. Second Edition. Fcap. 8vo. Cloth, price 4s. 6d.

KING (Edward).
Echoes from the Orient. With Miscellaneous Poems. Small crown 8vo. Cloth, price 3s. 6d.

KINGSLEY (Charles), M.A.
Letters and Memories of his Life. Edited by his WIFE. With 2 Steel engraved Portraits and numerous Illustrations on Wood, and a Facsimile of his Handwriting. Thirteenth Edition. 2 vols. Demy 8vo. Cloth, price 36s.
** Also the ninth Cabinet Edition in 2 vols. Crown 8vo. Cloth, price 12s.
All Saints' Day and other Sermons. Second Edition. Crown 8vo. Cloth, 7s. 6d.
True Words for Brave Men: a Book for Soldiers' and Sailors' Libraries. Eighth Edition. Crown 8vo. Cloth, price 2s. 6d.

KNIGHT (Professor W.).
Studies in Philosophy and Literature. Large post 8vo. Cloth, price 7s. 6d.

KNOX (Alexander A.).
The New Playground: or, Wanderings in Algeria. Large crown 8vo. Cloth, price 10s. 6d.

LACORDAIRE (Rev. Père).
Life: Conferences delivered at Toulouse. A New and Cheaper Edition. Crown 8vo. Cloth, price 3s. 6d.

LAIRD-CLOWES (W.).
Love's Rebellion: a Poem. Fcap. 8vo. Cloth, price 3s. 6d.

LAMONT (Martha MacDonald).
The Gladiator: A Life under the Roman Empire in the beginning of the Third Century. With four Illustrations by H. M. Paget. Extra fcap. 8vo. Cloth, price 3s. 6d.

LANG (A.).
XXII Ballades in Blue China. Elzevir. 8vo. Parchment, price 3s. 6d.

LAYMANN (Capt.).
The Frontal Attack of Infantry. Translated by Colonel Edward Newdigate. Crown 8vo. Cloth, price 2s. 6d.

LEANDER (Richard).
Fantastic Stories. Translated from the German by Paulina B. Granville. With Eight full-page Illustrations by M. E. Fraser-Tytler. Crown 8vo. Cloth, price 5s.

LEE (Rev. F. G.), D.C.L.
The Other World; or, Glimpses of the Supernatural. 2 vols. A New Edition. Crown 8vo. Cloth, price 15s.

LEE (Holme).
Her Title of Honour. A Book for Girls. New Edition. With a Frontispiece. Crown 8vo. Cloth, price 5s.

LEIGHTON (Robert).
Records and other Poems. With Portrait. Small crown 8vo. Cloth, price 7s. 6d.

LEWIS (Edward Dillon).
A Draft Code of Criminal Law and Procedure. Demy 8vo. Cloth, price 21s.

LEWIS (Mary A.).
A Rat with Three Tales. New and cheaper edition. With Four Illustrations by Catherine F. Frere. Crown 8vo. Cloth, price 3s. 6d.

LINDSAY (W. Lauder), M.D., &c.
Mind in the Lower Animals in Health and Disease. 2 vols. Demy 8vo. Cloth, price 32s.

LLOYD (Francis) and Charles Tebbitt.
Extension of Empire Weakness? Deficits Ruin? With a Practical Scheme for the Reconstruction of Asiatic Turkey. Small crown 8vo. Cloth, price 3s. 6d.

LOCKER (F.).
London Lyrics. A New and Revised Edition, with Additions and a Portrait of the Author. Crown 8vo. Cloth, elegant, price 6s.
Also, a Cheaper Edition. Fcap 8vo. Cloth, price 2s. 6d.

LOKI.
The New Werther. Small crown 8vo. Cloth, price 2s. 6d.

LONSDALE (Margaret).
Sister Dora. A Biography, with Portrait engraved on steel by C. H. Jeens, and one illustration. Twelfth edition. Crown 8vo. Cloth, price 6s.

LORIMER (Peter), D.D.
John Knox and the Church of England: His Work in her Pulpit, and his Influence upon her Liturgy, Articles, and Parties. Demy 8vo. Cloth, price 12s.

John Wiclif and his English Precursors, by Gerhard Victor Lechler. Translated from the German, with additional Notes. 2 vols. Demy 8vo. Cloth, price 21s.

Love's Gamut and other Poems. Small crown 8vo. Cloth, price 3s. 6d.

Love Sonnets of Proteus. With frontispiece by the Author. Elzevir 8vo. Cloth, price 5s.

LOWNDES (Henry).
Poems and Translations. Crown 8vo. Cloth, price 6s.

LUMSDEN (Lieut.-Col. H. W.).
Beowulf. An Old English Poem. Translated into modern rhymes. Small crown 8vo. Cloth, price 5s.

MAC CLINTOCK (L.).
Sir Spangle and the Dingy Hen. Illustrated. Square crown 8vo., price 2s. 6d.

MACDONALD (G.).
Malcolm. With Portrait of the Author engraved on Steel. Fourth Edition. Crown 8vo. Price 6s.

The Marquis of Lossie. Second Edition. Crown 8vo. Cloth, price 6s.

St. George and St. Michael. Second Edition. Crown 8vo. Cloth, 6s.

MACKENNA (S. J.).
Plucky Fellows. A Book for Boys. With Six Illustrations. Fourth Edition. Crown 8vo. Cloth, price 3s. 6d.

At School with an Old Dragoon. With Six Illustrations. Second Edition. Crown 8vo. Cloth, price 5s.

MACLACHLAN (Mrs.).
Notes and Extracts on Everlasting Punishment and Eternal Life, according to Literal Interpretation. Small crown 8vo. Cloth, price 3s. 6d.

MACLEAN (Charles Donald).
Latin and Greek Verse Translations. Small crown 8vo. Cloth, price 2s.

MACNAUGHT (Rev. John).
Cœna Domini: An Essay on the Lord's Supper, its Primitive Institution, Apostolic Uses, and Subsequent History. Demy 8vo. Cloth, price 14s.

MAGNUS (Mrs.).
About the Jews since Bible Times. From the Babylonian exile till the English Exodus. Small crown 8vo. Cloth, price 5s.

MAGNUSSON (Eirikr), M.A., and PALMER (E.H.), M.A.
Johan Ludvig Runeberg's Lyrical Songs, Idylls and Epigrams. Fcap. 8vo. Cloth, price 5s.

MAIR (R. S.), M.D., F.R.C.S.E.
The Medical Guide for Anglo-Indians. Being a Compendium of Advice to Europeans in India, relating to the Preservation and Regulation of Health. With a Supplement on the Management of Children in India. Second Edition. Crown 8vo. Limp cloth, price 3s. 6d.

MALDEN (H. E. and E. E.)
Princes and Princesses. Illustrated. Small crown 8vo. Cloth, price 2s. 6d.

MANNING (His Eminence Cardinal).
The True Story of the Vatican Council. Crown 8vo. Cloth, price 5s.

Marie Antoinette: a Drama. Small crown 8vo. Cloth, price 5s.

MARKHAM (Capt. Albert Hastings), R.N.
The Great Frozen Sea. A Personal Narrative of the Voyage of the "Alert" during the Arctic Expedition of 1875-6. With six full-page Illustrations, two Maps, and twenty-seven Woodcuts. Fourth and cheaper edition. Crown 8vo. Cloth, price 6s.

A Polar Reconnaissance: being the Voyage of the "Isbjorn" to Novaya Zemlya in 1879. With 10 Illustrations. Demy 8vo. Cloth, price 16s.

Master Bobby: a Tale. By the Author of "Christina North." With Illustrations by E. H. Bell. Extra fcap. 8vo. Cloth, price 3s. 6d.

MASTERMAN (J.).
Half-a-dozen Daughters. With a Frontispiece. Crown 8vo. Cloth, price 3s. 6d.

McGRATH (Terence).
Pictures from Ireland. New and cheaper edition. Crown 8vo. Cloth, price 2s.

MEREDITH (George).
The Egoist. A Comedy in Narrative. 3 vols. Crown 8vo. Cloth.
*** Also a Cheaper Edition, with Frontispiece. Crown 8vo. Cloth, price 6s.

MEREDITH (George)— *continued*.
The Ordeal of Richard Feverel. A History of Father and Son. In one vol. with Frontispiece. Crown 8vo. Cloth, price 6s.

MERRITT (Henry).
Art - Criticism and Romance. With Recollections, and Twenty-three Illustrations in *eau-forte*, by Anna Lea Merritt. Two vols. Large post 8vo. Cloth, 25s.

MIDDLETON (The Lady).
Ballads. Square 16mo. Cloth, price 3s. 6d.

MILLER (Edward).
The History and Doctrines of Irvingism; or, the so-called Catholic and Apostolic Church. 2 vols. Large post 8vo. Cloth, price 25s.

The Church in Relation to the State. Crown 8vo. Cloth, price 7s. 6d.

MILNE (James).
Tables of Exchange for the Conversion of Sterling Money into Indian and Ceylon Currency, at Rates from 1s. 8d. to 2s. 3d. per Rupee. Second Edition. Demy 8vo. Cloth, price £2 2s.

MINCHIN (J. G.).
Bulgaria since the War. Notes of a Tour in the Autumn of 1879. Small crown 8vo. Cloth, price 3s. 6d.

MOCKLER (E.).
A Grammar of the Baloochee Language, as it is spoken in Makran (Ancient Gedrosia), in the Persia-Arabic and Roman characters. Fcap. 8vo. Cloth, price 5s.

MOFFAT (Robert Scott).
The Economy of Consumption; an Omitted Chapter in Political Economy, with special reference to the Questions of Commercial Crises and the Policy of Trades Unions; and with Reviews of the Theories of Adam Smith, Ricardo, J. S. Mill, Fawcett, &c. Demy 8vo. Cloth, price 18s.

MOFFAT (Robert Scott)—continued.

The Principles of a Time Policy: being an Exposition of a Method of Settling Disputes between Employers and Employed in regard to Time and Wages, by a simple Process of Mercantile Barter, without recourse to Strikes or Locks-out. Reprinted from "The Economy of Consumption," with a Preface and Appendix containing Observations on some Reviews of that book, and a Re-criticism of the Theories of Ricardo and J. S. Mill on Rent, Value, and Cost of Production. Demy 8vo. Cloth, price 3s. 6d.

MOLTKE (Field-Marshal Von).
Letters from Russia. Translated by Robina Napier. Crown 8vo. Cloth, price 6s.

Notes of Travel. Being Extracts from the Journals of. Crown 8vo. Cloth, price 6s.

Monmouth: A Drama, of which the Outline is Historical. Dedicated by permission to Mr. Henry Irving. Small crown 8vo. Cloth, price 5s.

MOORE (Mrs. Bloomfield).
Gondaline's Lesson. The Warden's Tale, Stories for Children, and other Poems. Crown 8vo. Cloth, price 5s.

MORELL (J. R.).
Euclid Simplified in Method and Language. Being a Manual of Geometry. Compiled from the most important French Works, approved by the University of Paris and the Minister of Public Instruction. Fcap. 8vo. Cloth, price 2s. 6d.

MORICE (Rev. F. D.), M.A.
The Olympian and Pythian Odes of Pindar. A New Translation in English Verse. Crown 8vo. Cloth, price 7s. 6d.

MORSE (E. S.), Ph.D.
First Book of Zoology. With numerous Illustrations. New and cheaper edition. Crown 8vo. Cloth, price 2s. 6d.

MORSHEAD (E. D. A.)
The Agamemnon of Æschylus. Translated into English verse. With an Introductory Essay. Crown 8vo. Cloth, price 5s.

MORTERRA (Felix).
The Legend of Allandale, and other Poems. Small crown 8vo. Cloth, price 6s.

My Old Portfolio. A Volume of Poems. Crown 8vo. Cloth, price 4s. 6d.

NAAKE (J. T.).
Slavonic Fairy Tales. From Russian, Servian, Polish, and Bohemian Sources. With Four Illustrations. Crown 8vo. Cloth, price 5s.

NEWMAN (J. H.), D.D.
Characteristics from the Writings of. Being Selections from his various Works. Arranged with the Author's personal approval. Third Edition. With Portrait. Crown 8vo. Cloth, price 6s.

** A Portrait of the Rev. Dr. J. H. Newman, mounted for framing, can be had. price 2s. 6d.

NICHOLAS (Thomas), Ph.D., F.G.S.
The Pedigree of the English People: an Argument, Historical and Scientific, on the Formation and Growth of the Nation, tracing Race-admixture in Britain from the earliest times, with especial reference to the incorporation of the Celtic Aborigines. Fifth Edition. Demy 8vo. Cloth, price 16s.

NICHOLSON (Edward Byron).
The Christ Child, and other Poems. Crown 8vo. Cloth, price 4s. 6d.

The Rights of an Animal. Crown 8vo. Cloth, price 3s. 6d.

The Gospel according to the Hebrews. Its Fragments translated and annotated, with a critical Analysis of the External and Internal Evidence relating to it. Demy 8vo. Cloth, price 9s. 6d.

NICOLS (Arthur), F.G.S., F.R.G.S.
Chapters from the Physical History of the Earth. An Introduction to Geology and Palæontology, with numerous illustrations. Crown 8vo. Cloth, price 5s.

NOAKE (Major R. Compton).
The Bivouac; or, Martial Lyrist, with an Appendix—Advice to the Soldier. Fcap. 8vo. Price 5s. 6d.

NOEL (The Hon. Roden).
A Little Child's Monument. Small crown 8vo. Cloth, price 3s. 6d.

NORMAN PEOPLE (The).
The Norman People, and their Existing Descendants in the British Dominions and the United States of America. Demy 8vo. Cloth, price 21s.

NORRIS (Rev. Alfred).
The Inner and Outer Life Poems. Fcap. 8vo. Cloth, price 6s.

Notes on Cavalry Tactics, Organization, &c. By a Cavalry Officer. With Diagrams. Demy 8vo. Cloth, price 12s.

Nuces: Exercises on the Syntax of the Public School Latin Primer. New Edition in Three Parts. Crown 8vo. Each 1s.
*** The Three Parts can also be had bound together in cloth, price 3s.

O'BRIEN (Charlotte G.).
Light and Shade. 2 vols. Crown 8vo. Cloth, gilt tops, price 12s.

Ode of Life (The).
Third Edition. Fcap. 8vo. Cloth, price 5s.

O'HAGAN (John).
The Song of Roland. Translated into English Verse. Large post 8vo. Parchment antique, price 10s. 6d.

O'MEARA (Kathleen).
Frederic Ozanam, Professor of the Sorbonne; His Life and Works. Second Edition. Crown 8vo. Cloth, price 7s. 6d.

Our Public Schools. Eton, Harrow, Winchester, Rugby, Westminster, Marlborough, The Charterhouse. Crown 8vo. Cloth, price 6s.

OWEN (F. M.).
John Keats. A Study. Crown 8vo. Cloth, price 6s.

OWEN (Rev. Robert), B.D.
Sanctorale Catholicum; or Book of Saints. With Notes, Critical, Exegetical, and Historical. Demy 8vo. Cloth, price 18s.

An Essay on the Communion of Saints. Including an Examination of the "Cultus Sanctorum." Price 2s.

Palace and Prison and Fair Geraldine. Two Tragedies, by the Author of "Ginevra" and the "Duke of Guise." Crown 8vo. Cloth, 6s.

PALGRAVE (W. Gifford).
Hermann Agha; An Eastern Narrative. Third and Cheaper Edition. Crown 8vo. Cloth, price 6s.

PALMER (Charles Walter).
The Weed: a Poem. Small crown 8vo. Cloth, price 3s.

PANDURANG HARI;
Or, Memoirs of a Hindoo. With an Introductory Preface by Sir H. Bartle E. Frere, G.C.S.I., C.B. Crown 8vo. Price 6s.

PARKER (Joseph), D.D.
The Paraclete: An Essay on the Personality and Ministry of the Holy Ghost, with some reference to current discussions. Second Edition. Demy 8vo. Cloth, price 12s.

PARR (Capt. H. Hallam).
A Sketch of the Kafir and Zulu Wars: Guadana to Isandhlwana, with Maps. Small crown 8vo. Cloth, price 5s.

The Dress, Horses, and Equipment of Infantry and Staff Officers. Crown 8vo. Cloth, price 1s.

PARSLOE (Joseph).
Our Railways: Sketches, Historical and Descriptive. With Practical Information as to Fares, Rates, &c., and a Chapter on Railway Reform. Crown 8vo. Cloth, price 6s.

PATTISON (Mrs. Mark).
The Renaissance of Art in France. With Nineteen Steel Engravings. 2 vols. Demy 8vo. Cloth, price 32s.

PAUL (C. Kegan).
Mary Wollstonecraft.
Letters to Imlay. With Prefatory Memoir by, and Two Portraits in *eau forte*, by Anna Lea Merritt. Crown 8vo. Cloth, price 6s.

Goethe's Faust. A New Translation in Rime. Crown 8vo. Cloth, price 6s.

William Godwin: His Friends and Contemporaries. With Portraits and Facsimiles of the Handwriting of Godwin and his Wife. 2 vols. Square post 8vo. Cloth, price 28s.

The Genius of Christianity Unveiled. Being Essays by William Godwin never before published. Edited, with a Preface, by C. Kegan Paul. Crown 8vo. Cloth, price 7s. 6d.

PAUL (Margaret Agnes).
Gentle and Simple: A Story.
2 vols. Crown 8vo. Cloth, gilt tops, price 12s.

*** Also a Cheaper Edition in one vol. with Frontispiece. Crown 8vo. Cloth, price 6s.

PAYNE (John).
Songs of Life and Death.
Crown 8vo. Cloth, price 5s.

PAYNE (Prof. J. F.).
Lectures on Education.
Price 6d.
II. Fröbel and the Kindergarten system. Second Edition.

A Visit to German Schools: Elementary Schools in Germany. Notes of a Professional Tour to inspect some of the Kindergartens, Primary Schools, Public Girls' Schools, and Schools for Technical Instruction in Hamburgh, Berlin, Dresden, Weimar, Gotha, Eisenach, in the autumn of 1874. With Critical Discussions of the General Principles and Practice of Kindergartens and other Schemes of Elementary Education. Crown 8vo. Cloth, price 4s. 6d.

PELLETAN (E.).
The Desert Pastor, Jean Jarousseau. Translated from the French. By Colonel E. P. De L'Hoste. With a Frontispiece. New Edition. Fcap. 8vo. Cloth, price 3s. 6d.

PENNELL (H. Cholmondeley).
Pegasus Resaddled. By the Author of "Puck on Pegasus," &c. &c. With Ten Full-page Illustrations by George Du Maurier. Second Edition. Fcap. 4to. Cloth elegant, price 12s. 6d.

PENRICE (Maj. J.), B.A.
A Dictionary and Glossary of the Ko-ran. With copious Grammatical References and Explanations of the Text. 4to. Cloth, price 21s.

PESCHEL (Dr. Oscar).
The Races of Man and their Geographical Distribution. Large crown 8vo. Cloth, price 9s.

PFEIFFER (Emily).
Quarterman's Grace, and other Poems. Crown 8vo. Cloth, price 5s.

Glan Alarch: His Silence and Song. A Poem. Second Edition. Crown 8vo. price 6s.

Gerard's Monument, and other Poems. Second Edition. Crown 8vo. Cloth, price 6s.

Poems. Second Edition. Crown 8vo. Cloth, price 6s.

Sonnets and Songs. New Edition. 16mo, handsomely printed and bound in cloth, gilt edges, price 5s.

PINCHES (Thomas), M.A.
Samuel Wilberforce: Faith —Service—Recompense. Three Sermons. With a Portrait of Bishop Wilberforce (after a Photograph by Charles Watkins). Crown 8vo. Cloth, price 4s. 6d.

PLAYFAIR (Lieut.-Col.). Her Britannic Majesty's Consul-General in Algiers.

Travels in the Footsteps of Bruce in Algeria and Tunis. Illustrated by facsimiles of Bruce's original Drawings, Photographs, Maps, &c. Royal 4to. Cloth, bevelled boards, gilt leaves, price £3 3s.

POLLOCK (Frederick).
Spinoza. His Life and Philosophy. Demy 8vo. Cloth, price 16s.

POLLOCK (W. H.).
Lectures on French Poets. Delivered at the Royal Institution. Small crown 8vo. Cloth, price 5s.

POOR (Laura E.).
Sanskrit and its kindred Literatures. Studies in Comparative Mythology. Small crown 8vo. Cloth, price 5s.

POUSHKIN (A. S.).
Russian Romance. Translated from the Tales of Belkin, &c. By Mrs. J. Buchan Telfer (née Mouravieff). Crown 8vo. Cloth, price 3s. 6d.

PRESBYTER.
Unfoldings of Christian Hope. An Essay showing that the Doctrine contained in the Damnatory Clauses of the Creed commonly called Athanasian is unscriptural. Small crown 8vo. Cloth, price 4s. 6d.

PRICE (Prof. Bonamy).
Currency and Banking. Crown 8vo. Cloth, price 6s.

Chapters on Practical Political Economy. Being the Substance of Lectures delivered before the University of Oxford. Large post 8vo. Cloth, price 12s.

Proteus and Amadeus. A Correspondence. Edited by Aubrey De Vere. Crown 8vo. Cloth, price 5s.

PUBLIC SCHOOLBOY.
The Volunteer, the Militiaman, and the Regular Soldier. Crown 8vo. Cloth, price 5s.

PULPIT COMMENTARY (The). Edited by the Rev. J. S. EXELL and the Rev. Canon H. D. M. SPENCE.

Ezra, Nehemiah, and Esther. By Rev. Canon G. Rawlinson, M.A.; with Homilies by Rev. Prof. J. R. Thomson, M.A., Rev. Prof. R. A. Redford, LL.B., M.A., Rev. W. S. Lewis, M.A., Rev. J. A. Macdonald, Rev. A. Mackennal, B.A., Rev. W. Clarkson, B.A., Rev. F. Hastings, Rev. W. Dinwiddie, LL.B., Rev. Prof. Rowlands, B.A., Rev. G. Wood, B.A., Rev. Prof. P. C. Barker, LL.B., M.A., and Rev. J. S. Exell. Third Edition. Price 12s. 6d.

PULPIT COMMENTARY (The) —*continued.*

1 Samuel. By the Very Rev. R. P. Smith, D.D. With Homilies by the Rev. Donald Fraser, D.D., Rev. Prof. Chapman, and Rev. B. Dale. Third Edition. Price 15s.

Genesis. By Rev. T. Whitelaw, M.A.; with Homilies by the Very Rev. J. F. Montgomery, D.D., Rev. Prof. R. A. Redford, M.A., LL.B., Rev. F. Hastings, Rev. W. Roberts, M.A. An Introduction to the Study of the Old Testament by the Rev. Canon Farrar, D.D., F.R.S.; and Introductions to the Pentateuch by the Right Rev. H. Cotterill, D.D., and Rev. T. Whitelaw, M.A. Third Edition. Price 15s.

Judges and Ruth. By Right Rev. Lord A. C. Hervey, D.D., and Rev. J. Morrison, D.D. With Homilies by Rev. A. F. Muir, M.A.; Rev. W. F. Adeney, M.A.; Rev. W. M. Statham; and Rev. Prof. J. R. Thomson, M.A. Second Edition. Super royal 8vo. Cloth, price 15s.

Joshua. By the Rev J. J. Lias, M.A. With Homilies by the Rev. S. R. Aldridge, LL.B., Rev. R. Glover, Rev. E. de Pressensé, D.D., Rev. J. Waite, Rev. F. W. Adeney, and an Introduction by the Rev. A. Plummer, M.A. Second Edition. Price 12s. 6d.

Punjaub (The) and North Western Frontier of India. By an old Punjaubee. Crown 8vo. Cloth, price 5s.

Rabbi Jeshua. An Eastern Story. Crown 8vo. Cloth, price 3s. 6d.

RAVENSHAW (John Henry), B.C.S.
Gaur: Its Ruins and Inscriptions. Edited with considerable additions and alterations by his Widow. With forty-four photographic illustrations and twenty-five fac-similes of Inscriptions. Super royal 4to. Cloth, 3l. 13s. 6d.

READ (Carveth).
On the Theory of Logic: An Essay. Crown 8vo. Cloth, price 6s.

Realities of the Future Life. Small crown 8vo. Cloth, price 1s. 6d.

REANEY (Mrs. G. S.).
Blessing and Blessed; a Sketch of Girl Life. New and cheaper Edition. With a frontispiece. Crown 8vo. Cloth, price 3s. 6d.
Waking and Working; or, from Girlhood to Womanhood. New and cheaper edition. With a Frontispiece. Crown 8vo. Cloth, price 3s. 6d.
Rose Guerney's Discovery. A Book for Girls, dedicated to their Mothers. Crown 8vo. Cloth, price 3s. 6d.
English Girls: their Place and Power. With a Preface by R. W. Dale, M.A., of Birmingham. Third Edition. Fcap. 8vo. Cloth, price 2s. 6d.
Just Anyone, and other Stories. Three Illustrations. Royal 16mo. Cloth, price 1s. 6d.
Sunshine Jenny and other Stories. Three Illustrations. Royal 16mo. Cloth, price 1s. 6d.
Sunbeam Willie, and other Stories. Three Illustrations. Royal 16mo. Cloth, price 1s. 6d.

RENDALL (J. M.).
Concise Handbook of the Island of Madeira. With plan of Funchal and map of the Island. Fcap. 8vo. Cloth, price 1s. 6d.

REYNOLDS (Rev. J. W.).
The Supernatural in Nature. A Verification by Free Use of Science. Second Edition, revised and enlarged. Demy 8vo. Cloth, price 14s.
Mystery of Miracles, The. By the Author of "The Supernatural in Nature." Crown 8vo. Cloth, price 6s.

RHOADES (James).
The Georgics of Virgil. Translated into English Verse. Small crown 8vo. Cloth, price 5s.

RIBOT (Prof. Th.).
English Psychology. Second Edition. A Revised and Corrected Translation from the latest French Edition. Large post 8vo. Cloth, price 9s.

RIBOT (Prof. Th.)—*continued.*
Heredity: A Psychological Study on its Phenomena, its Laws, its Causes, and its Consequences. Large crown 8vo. Cloth, price 9s.

RINK (Chevalier Dr. Henry).
Greenland: Its People and its Products. By the Chevalier Dr. HENRY RINK, President of the Greenland Board of Trade. With sixteen Illustrations, drawn by the Eskimo, and a Map. Edited by Dr. ROBERT BROWN. Crown 8vo. Price 10s. 6d.

ROBERTSON (The Late Rev. F. W.), M.A., of Brighton.
The Human Race, and other Sermons preached at Cheltenham, Oxford, and Brighton. Second Edition. Large post 8vo. Cloth, price 7s. 6d.
Notes on Genesis. New and cheaper Edition. Crown 8vo., price 3s. 6d.
Sermons. Four Series. Small crown 8vo. Cloth, price 3s. 6d. each.
Expository Lectures on St. Paul's Epistles to the Corinthians. A New Edition. Small crown 8vo. Cloth, price 5s.
Lectures and Addresses, with other literary remains. A New Edition. Crown 8vo. Cloth, price 5s.
An Analysis of Mr. Tennyson's "In Memoriam." (Dedicated by Permission to the Poet-Laureate.) Fcap. 8vo. Cloth, price 2s.
The Education of the Human Race. Translated from the German of Gotthold Ephraim Lessing. Fcap. 8vo. Cloth, price 2s. 6d.
Life and Letters. Edited by the Rev. Stopford Brooke, M.A., Chaplain in Ordinary to the Queen.
I. 2 vols., uniform with the Sermons. With Steel Portrait. Crown 8vo. Cloth, price 7s. 6d.
II. Library Edition, in Demy 8vo., with Portrait. Cloth, price 12s.
III. A Popular Edition, in one vol. Crown 8vo. Cloth, price 6s.

The above Works can also be had half-bound in morocco.

*** A Portrait of the late Rev. F. W. Robertson, mounted for framing, can be had, price 2s. 6d.

C. Kegan Paul & Co.'s Publications. 25

ROBINSON (A. Mary F.).
A Handful of Honeysuckle. Fcap. 8vo. Cloth, price 3s. 6d.

RODWELL (G. F.), F.R.A.S., F.C.S.
Etna: a History of the Mountain and its Eruptions. With Maps and Illustrations. Square 8vo. Cloth, price 9s.

ROSS (Mrs. E.), ("Nelsie Brook").
Daddy's Pet. A Sketch from Humble Life. With Six Illustrations. Royal 16mo. Cloth, price 1s.

ROSS (Alexander), D.D.
Memoir of Alexander Ewing, Bishop of Argyll and the Isles. Second and Cheaper Edition. Demy 8vo. Cloth, price 10s. 6d.

SADLER (S. W.), R.N.
The African Cruiser. A Midshipman's Adventures on the West Coast. With Three Illustrations. Second Edition. Crown 8vo. Cloth, price 3s. 6d.

SALTS (Rev. Alfred), LL.D.
Godparents at Confirmation. With a Preface by the Bishop of Manchester. Small crown 8vo. Cloth, limp, price 2s.

SAMUEL (Sydney Montagu).
Jewish Life in the East. Small crown 8vo. Cloth, price 3s. 6d.

Sappho. A Dream. By the Author of "Palace and Prison," &c. Crown 8vo. Cloth, price 3s. 6d.

SAUNDERS (Katherine).
Gideon's Rock, and other Stories. Crown 8vo. Cloth, price 6s.
Joan Merryweather, and other Stories. Crown 8vo. Cloth, price 6s.
Margaret and Elizabeth. A Story of the Sea. Crown 8vo. Cloth, price 6s.

SAUNDERS (John).
Israel Mort, Overman: A Story of the Mine. Cr. 8vo. Price 6s.
Hirell. With Frontispiece. Crown 8vo. Cloth, price 3s. 6d.
Abel Drake's Wife. With Frontispiece. Crown 8vo. Cloth, price 3s. 6d.

SAYCE (Rev. Archibald Henry).
Introduction to the Science of Language. Two vols., large post 8vo. Cloth, price 25s.

SCHELL (Maj. von).
The Operations of the First Army under Gen. von Goeben. Translated by Col. C. H. von Wright. Four Maps. Demy 8vo. Cloth, price 9s.

The Operations of the First Army under Gen. von Steinmetz. Translated by Captain E. O. Hollist. Demy 8vo. Cloth, price 10s. 6d.

SCHELLENDORF (Maj.-Gen. B. von).
The Duties of the General Staff. Translated from the German by Lieutenant Hare. Vol. I. Demy 8vo. Cloth, 10s. 6d.

SCHERFF (Maj. W. von).
Studies in the New Infantry Tactics. Parts I. and II. Translated from the German by Colonel Lumley Graham. Demy 8vo. Cloth, price 7s. 6d.

Scientific Layman. The New Truth and the Old Faith: are they Incompatible? Demy 8vo. Cloth, price 10s. 6d.

SCOONES (W. Baptiste).
Four Centuries of English Letters. A Selection of 350 Letters by 150 Writers from the period of the Paston Letters to the Present Time. Edited and arranged by. Large crown 8vo. Cloth, price 9s.

SCOTT (Leader).
A Nook in the Apennines: A Summer beneath the Chestnuts. With Frontispiece, and 27 Illustrations in the Text, chiefly from Original Sketches. Crown 8vo. Cloth, price 7s. 6d.

SCOTT (Robert H.).
Weather Charts and Storm Warnings. Illustrated. Second Edition. Crown 8vo. Cloth, price 3s. 6d.

Seeking his Fortune, and other Stories. With Four Illustrations. New and cheaper Edition. Crown 8vo. Cloth, price 2s. 6d.

SENIOR (N. W.).
Alexis De Tocqueville.
Correspondence and Conversations with Nassau W. Senior, from 1833 to 1859. Edited by M. C. M. Simpson. 2 vols. Large post 8vo. Cloth, price 21s.

Sermons to Naval Cadets. Preached on board H.M.S. "Britannia." Small crown 8vo. Cloth, price 3s. 6d.

Seven Autumn Leaves from Fairyland. Illustrated with Nine Etchings. Square crown 8vo. Cloth, price 3s. 6d.

SHADWELL (Maj.-Gen.), C.B.
Mountain Warfare. Illustrated by the Campaign of 1799 in Switzerland. Being a Translation of the Swiss Narrative compiled from the Works of the Archduke Charles, Jomini, and others. Also of Notes by General H. Dufour on the Campaign of the Valtelline in 1635. With Appendix, Maps, and Introductory Remarks. Demy 8vo. Cloth, price 16s.

SHAKSPEARE (Charles).
Saint Paul at Athens: Spiritual Christianity in Relation to some Aspects of Modern Thought. Nine Sermons preached at St. Stephen's Church, Westbourne Park. With Preface by the Rev. Canon FARRAR. Crown 8vo. Cloth, price 5s.

SHAW (Major Wilkinson).
The Elements of Modern Tactics. Practically applied to English Formations. With Twenty-five Plates and Maps. S cond and cheaper Edition. Small crown 8vo. Cloth, price 9s.
*** The Second Volume of "Military Handbooks for Officers and Non-commissioned Officers." Edited by Lieut.-Col. C. B. Brackenbury, R.A., A.A.G.

SHAW (Flora L.).
Castle Blair: a Story of Youthful Lives. 2 vols. Crown 8vo. Cloth, gilt tops, price 12s. Also, an dition in one vol. Crown 8vo. 6s.

SHELLEY (Lady).
Shelley Memorials from Authentic Sources. With (now first printed) an Essay on Christianity by Percy Bysshe Shelley. With Portrait. Third Edition. Crown 8vo. Cloth, price 5s.

SHELLEY (Percy Bysshe).
Poems selected from. Dedicated to Lady Shelley. With Preface by Richard Garnett. Printed on hand-made paper. With miniature frontispiece. Elzevir. 8vo., limp parchment antique. Price 6s., vellum 7s. 6d.

SHERMAN (Gen. W. T.).
Memoirs of General W. T. Sherman, Commander of the Federal Forces in the American Civil War. By Himself. 2 vols. With Map. Demy 8vo Cloth, price 24s. *Copyright English Edition.*

SHILLITO (Rev. Joseph).
Womanhood: its Duties, Temptations, and Privileges. A Book for Young Women. Second Edition. Crown 8vo. Price 3s. 6d.

SHIPLEY (Rev. Orby), M.A.
Principles of the Faith in Relation to Sin. Topics for Thought in Times of Retreat. Eleven Addresses. With an Introduction on the neglect of Dogmatic Theology in the Church of England, and a Postscript on his leaving the Church of England. Demy 8vo. Cloth, price 12s.

Church Tracts, or Studies in Modern Problems. By various Writers. 2 vols. Crown 8vo. Cloth, price 5s. each.

Sister Augustine, Superior of the Sisters of Charity at the St. Johannis Hospital at Bonn. Authorized Translation by Hans Tharau from the German Memorials of Amalie von Lasaulx. Second edition. Large crown 8vo. Cloth, price 7s. 6d.

SMITH (Edward), M.D., LL.B., F.R.S.
Health and Disease, as Influenced by the Daily, Seasonal, and other Cyclical Changes in the Human System. A New Edition. Post 8vo. Cloth, price 7s. 6d.

Practical Dietary for Families, Schools, and the Labouring Classes. A New Edition. Post 8vo. Cloth, price 3s. 6d.

Tubercular Consumption in its Early and Remediable Stages. Second Edition. Crown 8vo. Cloth, price 6s.

Songs of Two Worlds. By the Author of "The Epic of Hades." Sixth Edition. Complete in one Volume, with Portrait. Fcap. 8vo. Cloth, price 7s. 6d.

Songs for Music. By Four Friends. Square crown 8vo. Cloth, price 5s. Containing songs by Reginald A. Gatty, Stephen H. Gatty, Greville J. Chester, and Juliana Ewing.

SPEDDING (James).
Reviews and Discussions, Literary, Political, and Historical, not relating to Bacon. Demy 8vo. Cloth, price 12s. 6d.

STAPFER (Paul).
Shakspeare and Classical Antiquity: Greek and Latin Antiquity as presented in Shakspeare's Plays. Translated by Emily J. Carey. Large post 8vo. Cloth, price 12s.

STEDMAN (Edmund Clarence).
Lyrics and Idylls. With other Poems. Crown 8vo. Cloth, price 7s. 6d.

STEPHENS (Archibald John), LL.D.
The Folkestone Ritual Case. The Substance of the Argument delivered before the Judicial Committee of the Privy Council. On behalf of the Respondents. Demy 8vo. Cloth, price 6s.

STEVENS (William).
The Truce of God, and other Poems. Small crown 8vo. Cloth, price 3s. 6d.

STEVENSON (Robert Louis).
An Inland Voyage. With Frontispiece by Walter Crane. Crown 8vo. Cloth, price 7s. 6d.

Travels with a Donkey in the Cevennes. With Frontispiece by Walter Crane. Crown 8vo. Cloth, price 7s. 6d.

Virginibus, Puerisque, and other Papers. Crown 8vo. Cloth, price 6s.

STEVENSON (Rev. W. F.).
Hymns for the Church and Home. Selected and Edited by the Rev. W. Fleming Stevenson. The most complete Hymn Book published. The Hymn Book consists of Three Parts :—I. For Public Worship.—II. For Family and Private Worship.—III. For Children.
*** *Published in various forms and prices, the latter ranging from 8d. to 6s. Lists and full particulars will be furnished on application to the Publishers.*

STOCKTON (Frank R.).
A Jolly Fellowship. With 20 Illustrations. Crown 8vo. Cloth, price 5s.

STORR (Francis), and TURNER Hawes).
Canterbury Chimes; or, Chaucer Tales retold to Children. With Illustrations from the Ellesmere MS. Extra Fcap. 8vo. Cloth, price 3s. 6d.

STRETTON (Hesba).
David Lloyd's Last Will. With Four Illustrations. Royal 16mo., price 2s. 6d.

The Wonderful Life. Thirteenth Thousand. Fcap. 8vo. Cloth, price 2s. 6d.

Through a Needle's Eye: a Story. 2 vols. Crown 8vo. Cloth, gilt top, price 12s.
*** Also a Cheaper Edition in one volume, with Frontispiece. Crown 8vo. Cloth, price 6s.

STUBBS (Lieut.-Colonel F. W.)
The Regiment of Bengal Artillery. The History of its Organization, Equipment, and War Services. Compiled from Published Works, Official Records, and various Private Sources. With numerous Maps and Illustrations. 2 vols. Demy 8vo. Cloth, price 32s.

STUMM (Lieut. Hugo), German Military Attaché to the Khivan Expedition.
Russia's advance Eastward. Based on the Official Reports of. Translated by Capt. C. E. H. VINCENT. With Map. Crown 8vo. Cloth, price 6s.

SULLY (James), M.A.
Sensation and Intuition.
Demy 8vo. Second Edition. Cloth, price 10s. 6d.
Pessimism : a History and a Criticism. Demy 8vo. Price 14s.

Sunnyland Stories.
By the Author of "Aunt Mary's Bran Pie." Illustrated. Small 8vo. Cloth, price 3s. 6d.

Sweet Silvery Sayings of Shakespeare. Crown 8vo. Cloth gilt, price 7s. 6d.

SYME (David).
Outlines of an Industrial Science. Second Edition. Crown 8vo. Cloth, price 6s.

Tales from Ariosto. Retold for Children, by a Lady. With three illustrations. Crown 8vo. Cloth, price 4s. 6d.

TAYLOR (Algernon).
Guienne. Notes of an Autumn Tour. Crown 8vo. Cloth, price 4s. 6d.

TAYLOR (Sir H.).
Works Complete. Author's Edition, in 5 vols. Crown 8vo. Cloth, price 6s. each.
Vols. I. to III. containing the Poetical Works, Vols. IV. and V. the Prose Works.

TAYLOR (Col. Meadows), C.S.I., M.R.I.A.
A Noble Queen : a Romance of Indian History. New Edition. With Frontispiece. Crown 8vo. Cloth. Price 6s.

Seeta. New Edition with frontispiece. Crown 8vo. Cloth, price 6s.

Tippoo Sultaun : a Tale of the Mysore War. New Edition with Frontispiece. Crown 8vo. Cloth, price 6s.

Ralph Darnell. New Edition. With Frontispiece. Crown 8vo. Cloth, price 6s.

The Confessions of a Thug. New Edition. With Frontispiece. Crown 8vo. Cloth, price 6s.

Tara : a Mahratta Tale. New Edition. With Frontispiece. Crown 8vo. Cloth, price 6s.

TEBBITT (Charles) and Francis Lloyd.
Extension of Empire Weakness? Deficits Ruin? With a Practical Scheme for the Reconstruction of Asiatic Turkey. Small crown 8vo. Cloth, price 3s. 6d.

TENNYSON (Alfred).
The Imperial Library Edition. Complete in 7 vols. Demy 8vo. Cloth, price £3 13s. 6d. ; in Roxburgh binding, £4 7s. 6d.
Author's Edition. Complete in 6 Volumes. Post 8vo. Cloth gilt ; or half-morocco, Roxburgh style :—
Vol. I. **Early Poems, and English Idylls.** Price 6s. ; Roxburgh, 7s. 6d.
Vol. II. **Locksley Hall, Lucretius, and other Poems.** Price 6s. ; Roxburgh, 7s. 6d.
Vol. III. **The Idylls of the King** (*Complete*). Price 7s. 6d.; Roxburgh, 9s.
Vol. IV. **The Princess, and Maud.** Price 6s.; Roxburgh, 7s. 6d.
Vol. V. **Enoch Arden, and In Memoriam.** Price 6s. ; Roxburgh, 7s. 6d.
Vol. VI. **Dramas.** Price 7s. ; Roxburgh, 8s. 6d.

Cabinet Edition. 12 vols. Each with Frontispiece. Fcap. 8vo. Cloth, price 2s. 6d. each.
CABINET EDITION. 12 vols. Complete in handsome Ornamental Case. 32s.

Pocket Volume Edition. 13 vols. In neat case, 36s. Ditto, ditto. Extra cloth gilt, in case, 42s.

The Royal Edition. With 25 Illustrations and Portrait. Cloth extra, bevelled boards, gilt leaves. Price 21s.

The Guinea Edition. Complete in 12 vols., neatly bound and enclosed in box. Cloth, price 21s. French morocco, price 31s. 6d.

The Shilling Edition of the Poetical and Dramatic Works, in 12 vols., pocket size. Price 1s. each.

C. Kegan Paul & Co.'s Publications. 29

TENNYSON (Alfred)—*continued.*

The Crown Edition. Complete in one vol., strongly bound in cloth, price 6s. Cloth, extra gilt leaves, price 7s. 6d. Roxburgh, half morocco, price 8s. 6d.

*** Can also be had in a variety of other bindings.

Original Editions:

Ballads and other Poems. Fcap. 8vo. Cloth, price 3s. 6d.

The Lover's Tale. (Now for the first time published.) Fcap. 8vo. Cloth, 3s. 6d.

Poems. Small 8vo. Cloth, price 6s.

Maud, and other Poems. Small 8vo. Cloth, price 3s. 6d.

The Princess. Small 8vo. Cloth, price 3s. 6d.

Idylls of the King. Small 8vo. Cloth, price 5s.

Idylls of the King. Complete. Small 8vo. Cloth, price 6s.

The Holy Grail, and other Poems. Small 8vo. Cloth, price 4s. 6d.

Gareth and Lynette. Small 8vo. Cloth, price 3s.

Enoch Arden, &c. Small 8vo. Cloth, price 3s. 6d.

In Memoriam. Small 8vo. Cloth, price 4s.

Queen Mary. A Drama. New Edition. Crown 8vo. Cloth, price 6s.

Harold. A Drama. Crown 8vo. Cloth, price 6s.

Selections from Tennyson's Works. Super royal 16mo. Cloth, price 3s. 6d. Cloth gilt extra, price 4s.

Songs from Tennyson's Works. Super royal 16mo. Cloth extra, price 3s. 6d.

Also a cheap edition. 16mo. Cloth, price 2s. 6d.

TENNYSON (Alfred)—*continued.*

Idylls of the King, and other Poems. Illustrated by Julia Margaret Cameron. 2 vols. Folio. Half-bound morocco, cloth sides, price £6 6s. each.

Tennyson for the Young and for Recitation. Specially arranged. Fcap. 8vo. Price 1s. 6d.

Tennyson Birthday Book. Edited by Emily Shakespear. 32mo. Cloth limp, 2s.; cloth extra, 3s.

*** A superior edition, printed in red and black, on antique paper, specially prepared. Small crown 8vo. Cloth extra, gilt leaves, price 5s.; and in various calf and morocco bindings.

In Memoriam. A new Edition, choicely printed on hand-made paper, with a Miniature Portrait in *eau forte* by Le Rat, after a photograph by the late Mrs. Cameron. Bound in limp parchment, antique, price 6s., vellum 7s. 6d.

The Princess. A Medley. Choicely printed on hand-made paper, with a miniature frontispiece by H. M. Paget and a tail-piece in outline by Gordon Browne. Limp parchment, antique, price 6s., vellum, price 7s.

Songs Set to Music, by various Composers. Edited by W. G. Cusins. Dedicated by express permission to Her Majesty the Queen. Royal 4to. Cloth extra, gilt leaves, price 21s., or in half-morocco, price 25s.

THOMAS (Moy).

A Fight for Life. With Frontispiece. Crown 8vo. Cloth, price 3s. 6d.

THOMPSON (Alice C.).

Preludes. A Volume of Poems. Illustrated by Elizabeth Thompson (Painter of "The Roll Call"). 8vo. Cloth, price 7s. 6d.

THOMSON (J. Turnbull).

Social Problems; or, an Inquiry into the Law of Influences. With Diagrams. Demy 8vo. Cloth, price 10s. 6d.

THRING (Rev. Godfrey), B.A.
Hymns and Sacred Lyrics.
Fcap. 8vo. Cloth, price 3s. 6d.

TODHUNTER (Dr. J.)
A Study of Shelley. Crown 8vo. Cloth, price 7s.
Alcestis : A Dramatic Poem.
Extra fcap. 8vo. Cloth, price 5s.
Laurella; and other Poems.
Crown 8vo. Cloth, price 6s. 6d.

TOLINGSBY (Frere).
Elnora. An Indian Mythological Poem. Fcap. 8vo. Cloth, price 6s.

Translations from Dante, Petrarch, Michael Angelo, and Vittoria Colonna. Fcap. 8vo. Cloth, price 7s. 6d.

TURNER (Rev. C. Tennyson).
Sonnets, Lyrics, and Translations. Crown 8vo. Cloth, price 4s. 6d.
Collected Sonnets, Old and New. With Preface by Alfred Tennyson; also some Marginal Notes by S. T. Coleridge, and a Critical Essay by James Spedding. Fcap. 8vo. Cloth, price 7s. 6d.

TWINING (Louisa).
Recollections of Workhouse Visiting and Management during twenty-five years. Small crown 8vo. Cloth, price 3s. 6d.

VAUGHAN (H. Halford), sometime Regius Professor of Modern History in Oxford University.
New Readings and Renderings of Shakespeare's Tragedies. 2 vols. Demy 8vo. Cloth, price 25s.

VILLARI (Prof.).
Niccolo Machiavelli and His Times. Translated by Linda Villari. 2 vols. Large post 8vo. Cloth, price 24s.

VINCENT (Capt. C. E. H.).
Elementary Military Geography, Reconnoitring, and Sketching. Compiled for Non-Commissioned Officers and Soldiers of all Arms. Square crown 8vo. Cloth, price 2s. 6d.

VYNER (Lady Mary).
Every day a Portion. Adapted from the Bible and the Prayer Book, for the Private Devotions of those living in Widowhood. Collected and edited by Lady Mary Vyner. Square crown 8vo. Cloth extra, price 5s.

WALDSTEIN (Charles), Ph. D.
The Balance of Emotion and Intellect: An Essay Introductory to the Study of Philosophy. Crown 8vo. Cloth, price 6s.

WALLER (Rev. C. B.)
The Apocalypse, Reviewed under the Light of the Doctrine of the Unfolding Ages and the Restitution of all Things. Demy 8vo. Cloth, price 12s.

WALTERS (Sophia Lydia).
The Brook : A Poem. Small crown 8vo. Cloth, price 3s. 6d.
A Dreamer's Sketch Book. With Twenty-one Illustrations by Percival Skelton, R. P. Leitch, W. H. J. Boot, and T. R. Pritchett. Engraved by J. D. Cooper. Fcap. 4to. Cloth, price 12s. 6d.

WARTENSLEBEN (Count H. von).
The Operations of the South Army in January and February, 1871. Compiled from the Official War Documents of the Head-quarters of the Southern Army. Translated by Colonel C. H. von Wright. With Maps. Demy 8vo. Cloth, price 6s.

The Operations of the First Army under Gen. von Manteuffel. Translated by Colonel C. H. von Wright. Uniform with the above. Demy 8vo. Cloth, price 9s.

WATERFIELD, W.
Hymns for Holy Days and Seasons. 32mo. Cloth, price 1s. 6d.

WATSON (William).
The Prince's Quest and other Poems. Crown 8vo. Cloth, price 5s.

C. Kegan Paul & Co.'s Publications. 31

WATSON Sir Thomas), Bart., M.D.
The Abolition of Zymotic Diseases, and of other similar enemies of Mankind. Small crown 8vo. Cloth, price 3s. 6d.

WAY (A.), M.A.
The Odes of Horace Literally Translated in Metre. Fcap. 8vo. Cloth, price 2s.

WEBSTER (Augusta).
Disguises. A Drama. Small crown 8vo. Cloth, price 5s.

WEDMORE (Frederick).
The Masters of Genre Painting. With sixteen illustrations. Crown 8vo. Cloth, price 7s. 6d

WELLS (Capt. John C.), R.N.
Spitzbergen—The Gateway to the Polynia; or, A Voyage to Spitzbergen. With numerous Illustrations by Whymper and others, and Map. New and Cheaper Edition. Demy 8vo. Cloth, price 6s.

Wet Days, by a Farmer. Small crown 8vo. Cloth, price 6s.

WETMORE (W. S.).
Commercial Telegraphic Code. Second Edition. Post 4to. Boards, price 42s.

WHITAKER (Florence).
Christy's Inheritance. A London Story. Illustrated. Royal 16mo. Cloth, price 1s. 6d.

WHITE (A. D.), LL.D.
Warfare of Science. With Prefatory Note by Professor Tyndall. Second Edition. Crown 8vo. Cloth, price 3s. 6d.

WHITNEY (Prof. W. D.).
Essentials of English Grammar for the Use of Schools. Crown 8vo. Cloth, price 3s. 6a.

WICKHAM (Capt. E. H., R.A.)
Influence of Firearms upon Tactics : Historical and Critical Investigations. By an OFFICER OF SUPERIOR RANK (in the German Army). Translated by Captain E. H. Wickham, R.A. Demy 8vo. Cloth, price 7s. 6d.

WICKSTEED (P. H.).
Dante : Six Sermons. Crown 8vo. Cloth, price 5s.

WILLIAMS (Rowland), D.D.
Life and Letters of, with Extracts from his Note-Books. Edited by Mrs. Rowland Williams. With a Photographic Portrait. 2 vols. Large post 8vo. Cloth, price 24s.

Stray Thoughts from the Note-Books of the Late Rowland Williams, D.D. Edited by his Widow. Crown 8vo. Cloth, price 3s. 6d.

Psalms, Litanies, Counsels and Collects for Devout Persons. Edited by his Widow. New and Popular Edition. Crown 8vo. Cloth, price 3s. 6d.

WILLIS (R.), M.D.
Servetus and Calvin : a Study of an Important Epoch in the Early History of the Reformation. 8vo. Cloth, price 16s.

William Harvey. A History of the Discovery of the Circulation of the Blood. With a Portrait of Harvey, after Faithorne. Demy 8vo. Cloth, price 14s.

WILLOUGHBY(The Hon. Mrs.).
On the North Wind — Thistledown. A Volume of Poems. Elegantly bound. Small crown 8vo. Cloth, price 7s. 6d.

WILSON (H. Schütz).
The Tower and Scaffold. A Miniature Monograph. Large fcap. 8vo. Price 1s.

Within Sound of the Sea. By the Author of "Blue Roses," "Vera," &c. Third Edition. 2 vols. Crown 8vo. Cloth, gilt tops, price 12s.

*** Also a cheaper edition in one Vol. with frontispiece. Crown 8vo. Cloth, price 6s.

WOINOVITS (Capt. I.).
Austrian Cavalry Exercise. Translated by Captain W. S. Cooke. Crown 8vo. Cloth, price 7s.

WOLLSTONECRAFT (Mary).
Letters to Imlay. With a Preparatory Memoir by C. Kegan Paul, and two Portraits in *eau forte* by Anna Lea Merritt. Crown 8vo. Cloth, price 6s.

WOLTMANN (Dr. Alfred), and WOERMANN (Dr. Karl).
History of Painting in Antiquity and the Middle Ages. Edited by Sidney Colvin. With numerous illustrations. Medium 8vo. Cloth, price 28s.; cloth, bevelled boards, gilt leaves, price 30s.

WOOD (Major-General J. Creighton).
Doubling the Consonant. Small crown 8vo. Cloth, price 1s. 6d.

WOODS (James Chapman).
A Child of the People, and other poems. Small crown 8vo. Cloth, price 5s.

Word was made Flesh. Short Family Readings on the Epistles for each Sunday of the Christian Year. Demy 8vo. Cloth, price 10s. 6d.

WRIGHT (Rev. David), M.A.
Waiting for the Light, and other Sermons. Crown 8vo. Cloth, price 6s.

YOUMANS (Eliza A.).
An Essay on the Culture of the Observing Powers of Children, especially in connection with the Study of Botany. Edited, with Notes and a Supplement, by Joseph Payne, F.C.P., Author of "Lectures on the Science and Art of Education," &c. Crown 8vo. Cloth, price 2s. 6d.

First Book of Botany. Designed to Cultivate the Observing Powers of Children. With 300 Engravings. New and Cheaper Edition. Crown 8vo. Cloth, price 2s. 6d.

YOUMANS (Edward L.), M.D.
A Class Book of Chemistry, on the Basis of the New System. With 200 Illustrations. Crown 8vo. Cloth, price 5s.

YOUNG (William).
Gottlob, etcetera. Small crown 8vo. Cloth, price 3s. 6d.

ZIMMERN (H.).
Stories in Precious Stones. With Six Illustrations. Third Edition. Crown 8vo. Cloth, price 5s.

www.ingramcontent.com/pod-product-compliance
Lightning Source LLC
Chambersburg PA
CBHW032107220426
43664CB00008B/1162